An exhibition at the National Portrait Gallery
October 16, 1980, to January 4, 1981
and at The Pennsylvania Academy of the Fine Arts
January 30 to April 19, 1981

MARVIN SADIK, *Director*
BEVERLY COX, *Curator of Exhibitions*
NELLO MARCONI, *Chief, Design and Production*
FRANCES STEVENSON WEIN, *Editor*

Benjamin West and His American Students

by

DORINDA EVANS

Published for the

NATIONAL PORTRAIT GALLERY

by the

SMITHSONIAN INSTITUTION PRESS

City of Washington

1980

© 1980 by Smithsonian Institution. All rights reserved.

Cover:
The American School, by Matthew Pratt, oil on canvas, 1765
The Metropolitan Museum of Art, Gift of Samuel P. Avery, 1897

Library of Congress Cataloging in Publication Data
Evans, Dorinda.
Benjamin West and his American students.

"[Published for] an exhibition at the National Portrait Gallery,
October 16, 1980, to January 4, 1981;
and at the Pennsylvania Academy of the Fine Arts,
January 30 to April 19, 1981,"
Bibliography: p.
Includes index.
1. Painting, American—Exhibitions.
2. Painting, Modern—17th-18th centuries—United States—Exhibitions.
3. Painting, Modern—19th century—United States—Exhibitions.
4. West, Benjamin, 1738-1820—Influence—Exhibitions.
I. National Portrait Gallery, Washington, D. C.
II. Pennsylvania Academy of the Fine Arts, Philadelphia.
III. Title.
ND207.E94   759.13'074'0153   80-14951

For sale by the Superintendent of Documents
United States Government Printing Office
Washington, D.C. 20402

Stock number: 047-000-000364-4

Contents

ACKNOWLEDGMENTS
7

LENDERS TO THE EXHIBITION
8

INTRODUCTION
11

BENJAMIN WEST
13

THE FIRST GENERATION (1760-1780)
24

Matthew Pratt
24

Abraham Delanoy
33

Charles Willson Peale
37

Joseph Wright
48

Gilbert Stuart
52

Ralph Earl
60

THE SECOND GENERATION (1780-1800)
71

John Trumbull
71

Mather Brown
74

Raphael Lamar West
103

Thomas Spence Duché
106

William Dunlap
111

George William West
112

Henry Sargent
113

Robert Fulton
116

THE THIRD GENERATION (1800-1820)
132

Washington Allston
132

Rembrandt Peale
142

Abraham G. D. Tuthill
144

Edward G. Malbone
145

Charles Bird King
146

Thomas Sully
151

Samuel Lovett Waldo
156

Samuel F. B. Morse
158

Charles Robert Leslie
161

Gilbert Stuart Newton
180

BIBLIOGRAPHY
191

INDEX
199

Acknowledgments

I am indebted to Anthony Garvan for first suggesting this topic as an exhibition theme, and to Allen Staley for his very helpful advice on several occasions. Various collectors played a role by providing information, and for this I am also grateful.

In doing research for the exhibition, I found the Archives of American Art, the Bicentennial Index of American Painting, the Catalog of American Portraits, and the Frick Art Reference Library especially useful. I would like to thank their staffs for assistance.

Ellen G. Miles and Frances Stevenson Wein made valuable suggestions about the text, while Beverly Cox performed the difficult task of coordinating the exhibition.

I want to express my gratitude to them particularly, and to Marvin Sadik most of all. He made this entire project possible by giving it his wholehearted support.

Dorinda Evans
January 1980

Lenders to the Exhibition

The Academy of Natural Sciences of Philadelphia
Addison Gallery of American Art, Phillips Academy
Amherst College, Mead Art Museum
The Athenaeum of Philadelphia
The Baltimore Museum of Art
Mrs. Stewart Taft Beach
The Beaverbrook Canadian Foundation, Beaverbrook Art Gallery
Eleanor Bliss
Library of the Boston Athenaeum
The estate of Walter Brandt
The John Carter Brown Library, Brown University
Canajoharie Library and Art Gallery
Carolina Art Association/Gibbes Art Gallery
The Cleveland Museum of Art
P. & D. Colnaghi & Co. Ltd.
The Connecticut Historical Society
Cooper-Hewitt Museum, Smithsonian Institution
Corcoran Gallery of Art
The Detroit Institute of Arts
Her Majesty Queen Elizabeth II
The Art History Department, Emory University
The Fine Arts Museums of San Francisco
Fogg Art Museum, Harvard University
The Folger Shakespeare Library
Fordham University Library
Glasgow Art Gallery and Museum
James M. Goode
Gordon S. Hargraves
The Historical Society of Pennsylvania
IBM Corporation
Independence National Historical Park
Dr. and Mrs. Henry C. Landon, III
Library of Congress
Henry H. Livingston
Maryland Department of General Services, Hall of Records and Artistic Property Commissions
Museum and Library of Maryland History/Maryland Historical Society
Massachusetts Historical Society
The Metropolitan Museum of Art
The Minneapolis Institute of Arts
Montclair Art Museum
The Pierpont Morgan Library
Museum of Early Southern Decorative Arts

Museum of Fine Arts, Boston
The Museum of Fine Arts, Houston
National Academy of Design
National Collection of Fine Arts, Smithsonian Institution
National Gallery of Art
National Maritime Museum, London
National Portrait Gallery, London
National Portrait Gallery, Smithsonian Institution
Nelson Gallery-Atkins Museum
The New-York Historical Society
University Art Gallery, State University of New York at Binghamton
New York State Historical Association
His Grace the Duke of Norfolk, CB.
The Pennsylvania Academy of the Fine Arts
Philadelphia Museum of Art
Pilgrim Hall
Portland Museum of Art
Princeton University Library
Private Collections
The Providence Athenaeum
Redwood Library and Athenaeum
James Ricau
Memorial Art Gallery of the University of Rochester
Royal Academy of Arts
Sabin Galleries
Salem Marine Society
Estate of Charles Coleman Sellers
Smith College Museum of Art
Somerville & Simpson Ltd
The J. B. Speed Art Museum
Diplomatic Reception Rooms, Department of State
The Tate Gallery
The Toledo Museum of Art
Trafalgar Galleries
Trinity College
The Virginia Museum of Fine Arts
Wadsworth Atheneum
Worcester Art Museum
Yale Center for British Art
Yale University Art Gallery

Introduction

This catalogue and exhibition focus primarily on Benjamin West's students rather than on the master himself. Hitherto, studies on West have not explored the extent and nature of his influence; and, when one considers that today he is regarded more highly as a teacher than as an artist, this is especially surprising.

Scholarly interest in West has burgeoned during the last decade, as evidenced by the Robert C. Alberts biography and the John Dillenberger and Jerry Meyer studies of West's religious paintings. Allen Staley shortly will publish a catalogue raisonné building on the unpublished researches of Helmut von Erffa. All this new activity follows a long period of neglect. West's work, which accorded so well with the particular taste of his period, has been much less highly esteemed by later generations. It is only recently, when the question has become not whether West was a second Raphael but whether his ingenuity placed him above most of his contemporaries, that he can be dealt with more objectively.

If ever the time was right for a study of West's students, it is certainly now, following his redemption. The obstacles, nevertheless, are considerable. What, for instance, constitutes a student? Because so many artists brought their work to West for criticism, particularly while he was president of England's Royal Academy, absolute criteria are difficult to establish. The problem is further complicated by the question of degree: some pupils chose to spend a long time with West, and consequently were more influenced by him than others who, keeping resolutely to their own ways, can more properly be said only to have been acquainted with him. Among this latter group were Abraham Delanoy and Henry Sargent, who nevertheless claimed to have studied with West—which in America was, of course, a source of prestige.

The only contemporary list of West's American students is that made by William Dunlap in his *Diary* and augmented in his *History of the Rise and Progress of the Arts of Design in the United States*.* The present exhibition will be limited to his roster, although some consideration will be given to those painters, such as James Earl, not included by Dunlap but usually accepted as members of West's circle.

* Dunlap lists Stuart, Wright, Trumbull, Brown, C.W. Peale, Ralph Earl, Fulton, Malbone, Sargent, Rembrandt Peale, Waldo, King, Sully, Leslie, Allston, Morse, Newton, and himself as students on the inside cover of Volume 26 of his memoirs published in 1931 as the *Diary of William Dunlap (1766-1839)*, New York, Vol. 2, p. 543n. In addition, he treats Delanoy, Pratt, Duché, Tuthill, Raphael West, and George William West as pupils in his *History of the Rise and Progress of the Arts of Design in the United States*.

Monographs have been written on nearly half of the students mentioned by Dunlap, including Charles Willson Peale, Gilbert Stuart, John Trumbull, Washington Allston, Edward G. Malbone, and Thomas Sully—but there is scant information on their training. Though this study can contribute only a few newspaper references and unpublished letters to the existing documentary evidence—especially on Thomas Duché, Mather Brown, Robert Fulton, Samuel F. B. Morse, Charles R. Leslie, and Samuel L. Waldo—it and the accompanying exhibition present the visual evidence for the first time: either the early work of these artists or a comparison of that done just prior to and following their contact with West.

Upon seeing the work of this group as a whole, one is first of all impressed with the wide range of achievement represented by the three generations of West's students. This should remind us of West's own versatility, which he was careful to develop—and which we tend to forget—coupled with the encouragement he gave to his students to pursue their own artistic inclinations. A number of his protégés influenced each other, and nearly all learned from their English contemporaries.

The quality of many of these young attempts to compete with the best pictures in England is striking. Because these artists turned to Benjamin West as their leader for more than half a century, and because they were themselves leaders in succeeding generations, West can justly be called the "father of American painting."

BENJAMIN WEST

In a letter of 1786 to Thomas Jefferson, George Washington expressed the most commonly held contemporary view of Benjamin West. He understood, he said, that "the taste, which has been introduced in painting by West [in London] is received with applause, and prevails extensively."[1]

The change in taste to which Washington was referring was brought about by West's celebrated depiction of *The Death of General Wolfe* [Figure 1]. One of England's greatest heroes, Wolfe had died on a battlefield in Quebec in 1759, during the French and Indian War, at the most dramatic moment when victory had just been assured. West's innovation, when he painted the scene in London in 1770, was to do it with an unusual emphasis on the moral content, with a new glamorization of heroic valor. He surprised his contemporaries by achieving his effect without drawing the traditional parallel with Greek and Roman times. That is, it was the custom for British artists who wished to stress

Figure 1.
The Death of General Wolfe
Benjamin West
Oil on canvas, 1771 version
153.7 x 245.1 cm. (60½ x 96½ in.)
Her Majesty Queen Elizabeth II

nobility of character, a trait identified with the ancients, to clothe their figures in antique costume whether the subject was contemporary or not. But, with a strong sense of his own destiny, West deliberately went against the prevailing tradition and used modern, military costume. If "I represent classical fictions," he reasoned, "how shall I be understood by posterity!"[2] When the large, finished painting was shown at the annual exhibition of the Royal Academy of Arts in 1771, its intense dramatization of a contemporary example of virtue was visually and morally electrifying. It was perceived as a success beyond all expectations; and, by departing from an artificial convention, West had set himself up as an innovator to be followed by other artists.

Benjamin West (1738-1820) was born in Springfield, Pennsylvania, the son of an innkeeper who had emigrated from England as a young man. His first real instruction in painting came from the English portrait painter, William Williams, whom he met in Philadelphia. From Williams, West, at about age ten, borrowed prints and books on art which included the theoretical works of Jonathan Richardson and Charles Alphonse Du Fresnoy.[3] Most of his lifelong attitudes on the supremacy of history painting and the importance of working from nature seem to have been formed at an early age by these authors. He concentrated as well on Plutarch, the Bible, and ancient history. Although he later received some instruction from the Reverend William Smith, a classical scholar and provost of the College at Philadelphia, he was largely self-taught, with an education limited to his special interests. West's ambition as an artist appears to have been unusually high, and he made at least two attempts while still a youth to break away from portrait painting and try historical subjects, in the manner of the great European masters: *The Trial of Susannah* (unlocated) and the *Death of Socrates* (private collection). The latter was partially copied from a frontispiece of the same scene in Volume Four of Charles Rollin's *Ancient History*, published in London in 1738–40. In his portraits and in works such as these, West was sufficiently encouraged by his friends so that he finally determined to save toward a trip abroad that would bring him improvement through study of the Old Masters. Several Philadelphia patrons contributed financially to the scheme, and, in 1760, he became the first American-born artist to travel to Italy.[4]

West's "imagination," according to his contemporary biographer, John Galt, writing in 1816, was "elevated in Italy to emulate the conceptions" of those celebrated artists "who have given a second existence to the great events of religion, history, and poetry."[5] West was particularly impressed by antique sculpture; by the sixteenth- and seventeenth-century paintings of Raphael, the Carracci, Guido Reni, and Nicolas Poussin; and by the contemporary neoclassical work of Pompeo Batoni and Anton Raphael Mengs, then the leading painters in Rome. With a gift for quick assimilation, he even produced a portrait of one of his companions, the English aristocrat Thomas Robinson (unlocated), towards the end of his three years in Rome, which was good enough to be mistaken for the work of Mengs. Such daring won him the approval of some of the city's most sophisticated connoisseurs. They began to regard him as a self-taught genius, untrained but capable of competing with the best in Rome. On Mengs's advice, he followed current theory in an eclectic approach to the Old Masters. Without becoming

Figure 2.
Angelica and Medoro
Benjamin West
Oil on canvas, 1763-64
92.1 x 71.8 cm. (36¼ x 28¼ in.)
University Art Gallery, State University of New York at Binghamton

an imitator of any one artist, West would try to combine the merits of several, such as Raphael's grace, Michelangelo's design, Correggio's soft shadows, and Titian's color.[6] The older painter encouraged West to travel through northern Italy and then to return and attempt more ambitious subjects.

From literary sources, West painted a *Cimon and Iphigenia* (unlocated) and a companion piece of *Angelica and Medoro* [Figure 2], which were well received by his friends in Rome. They were small compositions portraying idealized lovers: the *Cimon* based on a scene in Boccaccio's *Decameron* and the *Angelica* taken from Ariosto's poem, *Orlando Furioso*. In a coincidence which carried importance for the future, the *Cimon* was commissioned for England's King George III by an agent assigned to make purchases for the Royal Collection.

Probably, as in the surviving *Angelica*, the figures were derived from antique prototypes. The emphasis in *Angelica* on subtle modeling, muted color, and clarity of form, achieved with nearly invisible brushwork, was the height of fashion in Rome.

At last, after three years, West decided that he would return to America "to cultivate," as he would put it, "in his native country that profession in which he had already acquired so much celebrity."[7] His route home included a circuitous excursion through France to England, where he was so warmly welcomed that he remained for the rest of his life.

The account of John Galt, written with West's approval, has a running theme of predestination. This was West's outlook, but he seems in fact to have been unusually fortunate. The friendships that he had developed in Italy, for instance, were crucial in gaining support from some of the most respected artists in London, among them Joshua Reynolds, who had himself studied in Rome. West was also blessed, upon his arrival in England, because an Italian training was the most fashionable kind. He was able to take up a position of leadership almost immediately, for there was no other artist in London in 1763 who could rival him in his chosen area. The majority of England's artists were portraitists, the rest mostly landscapists. But it was in the category of the depiction of multi-figured scenes from the Bible, mythology, and history that one's ability could most truly be tested against the revered Old Masters. The field, above all, required imagination, a judicious choice of subject, a knowledge of the past, and a background, like West's, conversant with precedents. The artist who succeeded appeared not only learned but also of a superior moral stature. His subjects, whether religious or heroic, had, so it was thought, an uplifting effect on the public. Thus, West's contemporaries would praise him as one who painted not just for a living but for the transmission of his own elevated sentiments.

West began to paint, without a commission and on speculation, subjects from classical mythology, which were exhibited both in his studio and at the annual exhibitions of the Society of Artists of Great Britain (for London had the enticement of a public forum), where they were much admired. At first, the commissions were for portraits, but, finally, he was engaged to paint such scenes as the *Parting of Hector and Andromache* (probably the version at the New-York Historical Society) for the Bishop of Bristol and the *Return of the Prodigal Son* (unlocated) for the Bishop of Worcester, both between 1765 and 1771. This was a breakthrough, because historical commissions at that time were rare. The English aristocracy patronized their own artists for portraits, but, for history pictures, they habitually looked abroad and bought old paintings.

West had the appeal of novelty. He was nothing less than miraculous because his origins were American; and his classical subject matter was an attraction in itself. With the recent excavations of the ancient Roman towns of Herculaneum and Pompeii, there was a growing interest in antiquity that was nostalgic and investigative as well as commercial. Italy was the focus of the fashionable "grand tour," for those Englishmen who could afford it, and the center of a tourist market in "antique" sculpture, whether the genuine article or the fake. Also, to whet the public's appetite, there were an increasing number of illustrated publications on Greek and Roman remains: Dawkins and Wood on their Greek finds at Palmyra and Baalbek in the 1750s, Stuart and Revett producing their first volume of the *Antiquities of Athens* in 1762, and Piranesi holding up the Roman end with *Le Antichità Romane* in 1756. Some authors were more aesthetically appreciative than archaeological, and expounded on the ideal beauty which was to be found only in the simplicity and grandeur of classical sculpture. The most influential of these was Mengs's friend, Johann Joachim Winckelmann, who stressed the moral or ennobling content of Greek sculpture, equating spiritual beauty with physical perfection, in his *Reflections on the Painting and Sculpture of the Greeks*, published in German in 1755 and first translated into English in 1765. This fascination with classical remains constituted part of a new movement, later called neoclassicism, which was basically a reaction against the vacuous content of the rococo period. There was a dissatisfaction with frivolous subject matter and complicated decorative effects which could be associated with decadence and with England's traditional enemy, France. Instead, the new mode preferred an expression of ideal morality, frequently with a simplicity and directness which, as in antique statuary, had a value proven by time.

West's earliest English paintings—including the 1770 version of *Agrippina Landing at Brundisium with the Ashes of Germanicus* [Figure 3], based upon a

Figure 3.
Agrippina Landing at Brundisium with the Ashes of Germanicus
Benjamin West
Oil on canvas, 1770, after the original of 1766
165 x 188 cm. (65 x 74 in.)
Philadelphia Museum of Art
Not in Washington

Figure 4.
Last Supper
Benjamin West
Oil on canvas, 1770, after the original of 1766
258.9 x 355.6 cm. (98 x 140½ in.)
Somerville & Simpson Ltd, London

sketch dated 1766—were in the new neoclassical style that he had learned in Rome: a smooth surface; strong, but fairly somber, local colors; sharp delineation throughout; and a carefully modulated chiaroscuro. *Agrippina* is arranged in a frieze-like fashion (except for the diagonal movement at the right) and, in fact, was inspired by the solemn processional reliefs on the ancient Ara Pacis, which West had copied, in Rome. The focus is on the stoic Agrippina, in mourning, and her story of conjugal devotion even after death. Carrying the ashes of her husband, she traveled from Syria to Rome in order to demand justice for his murder which had been monstrously instigated, she believed, by the Emperor Tiberius. The subject was chosen from the *Annals* of Tacitus by the Archbishop of York, who was so pleased with the result that he brought West to the attention of the king. George III commissioned, in 1768, a companion piece of *The Departure of Regulus* [Figure 24] and followed this honor with West's appointment, in 1772, as "Historical Painter to the King." Although West was a charter member of the Royal Academy of Arts, which superseded the Society of Artists, in 1768, it was his growing friendship with young George III, who was his own age, that brought him the most prestige. Indeed he was wholly occupied, until the turn of the century, with assignments from the monarch.

When George III ascended the throne in 1760, there was the hope that his reign, unlike his grandfather's, would be a boon to the arts and that London might become the city that Rome once was. Certainly the new king set a higher moral tone, consistent with current romantic notions of ancient stoicism, and his reign opened with a burst of picture collecting which included Flemish, Dutch, and particularly Italian paintings.[8]

He intended, of course, to redecorate the royal apartments, and West was ever ready with ideas on uplifting subjects that could be grouped thematically. The king's copy of the popular *Death of General Wolfe*, they decided, was to be treated as a centerpiece for a series to include death scenes from classical and medieval times. Likewise, the sovereign and the painter agreed that the state rooms in Windsor Castle would benefit from a cycle of eight pictures on the life of Edward III. West's projects at Windsor included a number of royal portraits, a large *Last Supper* [Figure 4; color, page 124], and designs for stained-glass windows in St. George's Chapel, ceiling motifs for the Queen's Lodge, and some decorations for entertainments. But the major commission, apparently approved in 1780, was for a series of huge canvases on the History of Revealed Religion—instances of the revelation of God's will in the Bible—to be placed in a private chapel which would be specially built for them in Windsor Castle. This, in its immensity as a collective statement, planned to include about thirty-five paintings, was the one enterprise that was closest to West's heart.

Second to this project, West's life's work centered on two important groups of religious painting: subjects from the *Book of Revelation* for William Beckford's medieval folly, Fonthill Abbey; and the gigantic exhibition pieces of West's last decade which encompassed *Christ Healing the Sick in the Temple* (first version, 1810, Tate Gallery; second, 1815 [Figure 5]), *Christ Rejected by the Jews* (1814 [Figure 6]), and the final version of *Death on a Pale Horse* (1817, Pennsylvania Academy of the Fine Arts). West and many of his contemporaries considered these late canvases the culmination of his career. Despite such a favorable judgment, however, all of his long-term projects ended in considerable disillusionment. The Beckford series and the Revealed Religion series were canceled before they could be completed. Beckford's financial reverses made it clear, by 1802, that there would never be a "Revelation Chamber," and West did not fare any better with his friend, George III, whose increasing fits of mental illness (porphyria) rendered his patronage worthless by 1810.

But West could look back on his career with satisfaction. Although he had been born an American, he received the highest honors ever given to an English artist. Upon being elected the second president of the Royal Academy in 1792, he was even offered a knighthood. This he refused, apparently partly because he hoped for better than a non-hereditary title and partly because his reaction would have an impressive effect when compared to that of his predecessor, Sir Joshua Reynolds.

West, handsome and affable, had a sense of mission which was greater than even his desire for personal gain. His exalted purpose and supreme confidence in his own ability were reassuring to his students. Fanny Burney, one of the local bluestockings, sized him up in her well-known diary, and, although her description is superficial (based, as it is, on only a few encounters), it has value as a fresh impression by a perceptive observer, which coincides with the published views of him. West spoke to her of his work with "frank praise and open satisfaction," she recorded, and "Yet all with a Simplicity that turned his self-commendation rather into candour than conceit." On a third meeting, in 1787, his conversation was the same, and she noted that "such language about his own per-

Figure 5.
Christ Healing the Sick in the Temple
Benjamin West
Oil on canvas, 1815
335.2 x 548.8 cm. (132 x 216 in.)
Pennsylvania Hospital, Philadelphia
Not in exhibition

formances" would, in another man, "be totally ridiculous . . . but there is, in Mr. West, a something of simplicity in manner, that makes his self-recommendation seem the result rather of an unaffected mind than of a vain or proud one."[9]

West excelled in composition, and no one, a competitor confessed, could "draw with more accuracy from his model."[10] Yet it was his subject matter, his variety of grand conceptions, that set him apart and attracted a following who believed that he was a second Raphael.

West's fame abroad, as well as in England, was magnified by the widespread distribution, beginning in about 1771, of engravings after his historical pictures. The quality and number of these prints, some of them of a large size (with an image, for instance, measuring 24½ by 17½ inches), provided perhaps the best possible advertisement of his ability. After West's death, another painter, Sir Martin Archer Shee, wrote: "Let the most prejudiced of those who are inclined to question his claims to the rank of a great artist examine the series of prints engraved from his works."[11] The most famous of these was William Woollett's 1776 engraving of *The Death of General Wolfe*. The popularity of this print brought the publisher, John Boydell, fifteen thousand pounds by 1790 and established a record which challenged emulation. Through this one engraving, West started a vogue for similar prints which helped to provide financial support for historical painting.

Even as West was just beginning in London, he started to attract other American artists as his protégés. In this way, he became a phenomenon unique in American art. With virtually no competition, London was the most prestigious art center in the English-speaking world, but her schools of art, most notably the Royal Academy after 1768, were classrooms for drawing. It was assumed that an artist would learn more specifically the rudiments of his chosen profession in some outside studio. West's position and willingness to help fellow-

Figure 6.
Christ Rejected by the Jews
Benjamin West
Oil on canvas, 1814
508 x 660.4 cm. (200 x 260 in.)
The Pennsylvania Academy of the Fine Arts, Philadelphia, Gift of Mrs. Joseph Harrison, Jr.
Not in Washington

colonials made his establishment the logical site for demonstrating painting techniques to Americans.

There is, throughout his career, a general consensus about him as a teacher and, on the whole, as a man. One of the most frequent first impressions, as his pupil Gilbert Stuart soon discovered, was that West was not an effective speaker. He would sometimes mispronounce words or naively misjudge his audience and go over elementary ideas in a monotonous fashion.

Yet Stuart also observed, late in life, that West was "the wisest man" he ever knew.[12] He referred, in the same sentence, to West's "goodness." It was this characteristic, a kindness and generosity, that, combined with experience, made his early instructor appear so wise. West's criticism of the work of others was usually astute, as when, many years later, he advised the budding English landscapist, John Constable, "Always remember, sir, that light and shadow never stand still." Taking up a piece of chalk, West added some secondary lights to the shadows in one of Constable's paintings and reminded him that his dark skies should resemble the darks of silver, not of lead. Constable knew enough to heed West's advice at a time when he took little criticism from anyone.[13]

West was also instinctively diplomatic. Thomas Lawrence recalled that when West disapproved of a painting, he was silent, "a most provoking silence."[14] This was accompanied by a "parental fondness" and "the gentle humanity of his nature," which must have been a welcome relief to the most sensitive of American neophytes.[15]

Part of West's appeal was his availability. Reynolds's student, James Northcote, wrote that when he first went to his master's house to paint, he discovered that the other pupils were absolute strangers to Reynolds's way of working and knew nothing about what colors and varnishes he used. Reynolds always painted in a room set apart from them and was so busy that his followers rarely saw him.[16] In contrast, one of West's last pupils, Charles Robert Leslie, claimed that no other instructor was so "accessible."[17] Another student, William Dunlap, expressed it this way: "He had no secrets or mysteries, he told all he knew."[18] West's later practice (probably in the 1770s as well) was to receive his pupils in the morning and advise them on their work before he began on his own.[19] At first, he undoubtedly gave some instruction in his methods of grinding and mixing pigments, the laying out of the palette, and the preparation of the canvas; but, later, a more experienced protégé would teach newcomers.

As Dunlap recognized, West emphasized the importance of working from nature to avoid some of the mannerisms that might be acquired by the constant copying of a few artists. "Work, night & day," he would tell them, "draw from the Antique, paint from nature. Study the masters but copy nature."[20] Then he would remind them that he had taught himself, in the wilderness, by observing nature and that if, instead, he had been exposed too young to the masters, he would not have been able to develop beyond them.

In his approach, West was considered "scientific" because his critical comments were nearly always given as the deduction of general truths from his observation of nature or the work of others. His friend, Sir George Beaumont, said in 1805 that West was " 'the most scientific artist that had appeared' since Poussin."[21] One must remember that the "Science of Painting" was really concerned with a knowledge of history painting or Old Masters, "for in Historical Compositions it is surely more than an Art."[22] West spoke of painting as the "refinement of science."[23] In Italy he had used his scientific methods to try to reproduce the luminosity of Titian's transparent colors and, after repeated attempts, he felt sure that he had uncovered the secret. The answer, he believed, was to paint with pure primary colors and then soften them afterwards by glazing with muted tints. Galt says that West "was not perfectly satisfied with its soundness as a rule, till many years after his arrival in London, and many unsuccessful experiments."[24] He painted in conformity with the rules that he had deduced, so that, "according to his theory," as one contemporary explained, "what he did was quite right."[25] "There is not a line or a touch in his pictures," wrote one student, "which he cannot account for on philosophical principles."[26]

As can be seen, West developed a kind of magnetic power because of his belief in his own success. In his enthusiasm, he told his aspirants from abroad what they were starved to hear: that the profession was a noble one, fit for kings; and he "conceived of painting as a mechanical or scientific process" which, to a large degree, could be taught to nearly anyone.[27] Compared to his English counterparts, West was unusual in his optimism and in the personal interest he took in his students, for he became a patient and generous benefactor in ways outside of pure instruction. He also encouraged his pupils to pursue their own bent, not to become his imitators; and, in this last respect, he showed a breadth of wisdom that made him a truly great teacher.

Notes

1. Mabel Munson Swan, *The Athenaeum Gallery, 1827-1873* (Boston: 1940), p. 163.

2. John Galt, *The Life of Benjamin West*, ed. Nathalia Wright (Gainesville, Fla.: 1960) reprint ed., pt. 2, p. 48.

3. Probably Jonathan Richardson, *An Essay on the Theory of Painting* (London: 1725); and Charles A. Du Fresnoy, *De Arte Graphica: The Art of Painting*, trans. John Dryden (London: 1695).

4. Possibly he was preceded by a Mr. Steele, the native of Maryland who in 1762 was reputed to have studied painting in Italy. Cf. Charles Coleman Sellers, *Charles Willson Peale* (New York: 1969), p. 30.

5. Galt, *Life of Benjamin West*, pt. 2, p. 17.

6. *Ibid.*, pt. 1, pp. 122 and 131. This is the course that West, later in 1773, recommended to Copley. Cf. Guernsey Jones, ed., *Letters and Papers of John Singleton Copley and Henry Pelham, 1739-1776* (New York: 1970) reprint ed., p. 194.

7. Galt, *Life of Benjamin West*, pt. 1, p. 143.

8. The Queen's Gallery, *George III: Collector and Patron* (London: 1974-75), pp. 3 and 5.

9. Unpublished section of Fanny Burney's diary, October 1786 and January 2, 1787, vol. 3, pp. 2364 and 2477, Berg Collection, The New York Public Library, New York, N.Y. For a similar opinion, see Allan Cunningham, *The Lives of the Most Eminent British Painters, Sculptors, and Architects* (London: 1830), p. 56; William Hazlitt, *Criticism on Art* (London: 1844), 2d ser., pp. 369-70; and Stephen Gwynn, *Memorials of an Eighteenth Century Painter (James Northcote)* (London: 1898), pp. 241-42.

10. Gwynn, *Memorials*, p. 239.

11. William Dunlap, *A History of the Rise and Progress of the Arts of Design in the United States* (New York: 1969), reprint ed., vol. 1, p. 97.

12. John Hill Morgan, *Gilbert Stuart and His Pupils* (New York: 1939), p. 84.

13. Graham Reynolds, *Constable, the Natural Painter* (New York: 1965), p. 28.

14. Letter, T. Lawrence to Joseph Farington, n.d., vol. 1, fol. 164, Lawrence Papers, Library of the Royal Academy, London.

15. William Paulet Carey, *Observations on the Probable Decline and Extinction of British Historical Painting* (London: 1825), p. 74.

16. Charles Robert Leslie and Tom Taylor, *Life and Times of Sir Joshua Reynolds* (London: 1865), vol. 1, p. 409.

17. Charles Robert Leslie, *Autobiographical Recollections by the Late Charles Robert Leslie, R.A.*, ed. Tom Taylor (London: 1860), p. 57.

18. William Dunlap, *Diary of William Dunlap (1766-1839)* (New York: 1931), vol. 2, p. 543.

19. Leslie, *Recollections*, p. 57.

20. Dunlap, *Diary*, vol. 2, p. 543.

21. *Joseph Farington's Diary*, microfilm (unpublished entry), December 15, 1805, The New York Public Library, New York.

22. Benjamin Ralph, *The School of Raphael: Or the Student's Guide to Expression in Historical Painting* (London: 1759), p. (1).

23. John Dillenberger, *Benjamin West: The Context of His Life's Work with Particular Attention to Paintings with Religious Subject Matter* (San Antonio, Tex.: 1977), p. 117.

24. Galt, *Life of Benjamin West*, pt. 1, p. 131.

25. Gwynn, *Memorials*, p. 241.

26. Edward Lind Morse, *Samuel F. B. Morse: His Letters and Journals* (Boston: 1914), vol. 1, p. 68.

27. William Hazlitt, quoted in Gwynn, *Memorials*, p. 241.

THE FIRST GENERATION
1760-1780

Matthew Pratt

In July of 1764, Matthew Pratt (1734-1805), the man who would be considered West's first American pupil, arrived in London. He came not as a student but as an escort for his cousin, the young and attractive Betsy Shewell, who was engaged to be married to Benjamin West. Pratt was to represent the Shewell family at the marriage ceremony. Undoubtedly he volunteered for the journey, for he was a practicing artist himself and certainly knew West, four years his junior, when they both were tyros together in Philadelphia.[1] He was, in fact, so eager to confirm the reports of West's advancement and to learn from West's experience that he left his wife and two young sons, one only nine months old, to undertake the voyage.

After the West-Shewell wedding, Pratt recalled that "We returned, to the City, where Mr. Benjn West had a very large elegant house, completely fitted up, to accommodate a very large family, and where he followed his occupation, in great repute, as a Historical & Portrait painter." Pratt joined the household in Castle Street, Leicester Fields. Provided with a room, he was given, as he said, "every good & kind office" that West "could bestow on me, as if I was his Father, friend and brother."[2] Pratt spent two-and-a-half years in London and eighteen months more in Bristol, where he practiced on his own before returning to Philadelphia in March of 1768.

Evidently, Pratt was especially interested in gaining from the expertise that his younger colleague had acquired in Italy. It was the custom to learn by copying, so Pratt began on West's copy of Correggio's *Madonna of St. Jerome* (Pratt's version [Figure 7]); West's *Venus and Cupid*, apparently the one exhibited at the Society of Artists in 1765; Guido Reni's painting of *Jupiter and Europa*, probably recommended by West; and some of West's portraits that Pratt selected as the best of his friend's work in this genre (all unlocated).

Only two of Pratt's portraits from the period before London are known: a likeness of his young wife [Figure 8], usually dated to the year of their marriage, 1760, and a copy (The American Scenic and Historic Preservation Society) of a 1761 engraving after Benjamin Wilson's portrait of Benjamin Franklin. Both of these exhibit a rather crude use of thick paint which seems to derive from his training, in an artisan tradition, under his uncle, James Claypoole, Sr., who advertised his versatility as a limner, house painter, and glazier all in one. Nowhere near as ambitious as West, Pratt, in Philadelphia days, had not even been averse

Figure 7.
Madonna of St. Jerome
Matthew Pratt
Oil on canvas, 1764/66
77.8 x 60 cm. (30⅝ x 23⅝ in.)
National Gallery of Art,
Washington, D.C., Gift of
Clarence Van Dyke Tiers, 1945

to repainting fire engines.[3] His first exhibited work, *A Fruit Piece* (unlocated), at the Society of Artists in 1765, was undoubtedly an extension of his past experience in ornamental painting. Perhaps his earliest London picture is the *Self-Portrait* [Figure 9] of about 1764. It may have been intended as a demonstration of Pratt's skill, since it shows him as an artist, looking up from sheets of drawing paper, with a rather confident expression, and holding a brass *porte-crayon*. Clearly he was learning to improve his drawing, and this was one of the ways in which West most helped him. While the broad treatment of the *Self-Portrait* relates it to his early style, the pose is more relaxed and facial features better integrated with the head than in his Philadelphia work.

25

Figure 8.
Elizabeth Moore (Mrs. Matthew Pratt)
Matthew Pratt
Oil on canvas, circa 1760
73.7 x 61 cm. (29 x 24 in.)
Private collection

It was not long before he began to assume the carefully modeled, more finished, and sharply defined neoclassical style associated with West, and with such esteemed English portraitists as Allan Ramsay who had also studied in Italy and was at the height of his powers. The smooth surface, with a minimum of visible "pencilling," that is typical of West in his handsome portrait of *Diana Mary Barker* [Figure 10], of 1766, is found in Pratt's companion likenesses of his hosts, *Benjamin West* and *Elizabeth Shewell* [Figures 11 and 12], which also show the new care he was taking with softer, more meticulous modeling of the pale flesh. From West, Pratt further acquired certain illusionistic skills, such as the use of a light behind a figure, as in the *Self-Portrait* and *Elizabeth Shewell*, in order to create a more convincing sense of space.

Pratt's more ambitious attempt, while in London, was both a public tribute

Figure 9.
Self-Portrait
Matthew Pratt
Oil on canvas, circa 1764
76.2 x 63 cm. (30 x 24¾ in.)
National Portrait Gallery,
Smithsonian Institution

to his young friend and an advertisement of his gift for teaching. Exhibited at the Society of Artists' annual in 1766, *The American School* [Figure 13; color, cover] was created as a showpiece and is the only known painting that Pratt deemed worthy of a signature and a date (1765). In subject and style, it resembles West's *Cricketers* [Figure 14], which was probably painted in 1763. Both were executed in the tradition of the English "conversation piece," in which a group of small, full-length figures are involved with each other, somewhat unconsciously, in what appears to be a daily activity. West is presented in his studio, standing at the left, dressed in green and wearing his tricorn hat in Quaker style, giving instruction on drawing to Pratt while the other students patiently await their turn. The figure at the right, in profile, before the canvas with Pratt's signature, has provoked some controversy and has been variously identified as Pratt or Abra-

Figure 10.
Diana Mary Barker
Benjamin West
Oil on canvas, 1766
94 x 83.8 cm. (37 x 33 in.)
The Minneapolis Institute of Arts,
Gift of James F. and Louise H. Bell in
Memory of James S. and Sallie M. Bell

ham Delanoy, an American who might have been in West's studio as early as this.[4] Delanoy's features are not known, but Pratt's are, and they do not resemble those represented here. The two boyish pupils behind are a puzzle as well. Apparently, by the spring of 1765, West had formed a school which included a number of young men, some English, who have since fallen into obscurity.

Pratt's picture is listed in the 1766 exhibition catalogue as "The American School" rather than the "School of West," the label under which it was shown in 1811 and again in 1838 in Philadelphia. In choosing his title, Pratt undoubtedly wanted to make West's studio seem unusual. Later the studio was commonly referred to by Americans who had studied there, like William Dunlap, as "The London School of Artists." This reference implies a mental association not just with West but the whole London experience. The distinction is instructive, since it infers that the impact of West's personality was not great. He did not dominate or dictate to his students. For Americans who had never been to London, however, such as the exhibition-goers in Philadelphia, it was the school of a single

Figure 11.
Benjamin West
Matthew Pratt
Oil on canvas, 1765
76.2 x 63.5 cm. (30 x 25 in.)
The Pennsylvania Academy of the Fine Arts, Philadelphia
Not in Washington

celebrity, "the famous Mr. West."

With a multi-figured subject, Pratt had an excuse to demonstrate his ability to master a complex composition. Visually and psychologically, there is a strong, central focus with the main colors carefully distributed, in the manner of West, to reinforce a sense of balance. His use of light and shade to emphasize crisp edges and leave others soft is convincingly done, and he has cleverly employed a background canvas to frame and dramatize the three-dimensional profile at the right. His style has become more fashionable, and he has learned tricks of illusion and composition; but his drawing of anatomy is, in this picture, still, at times, sadly naive.

Pratt's manner so approached that of his teacher that, many years after he returned to Philadelphia, the young artist Thomas Sully mistook *The American*

Figure 12.
*Elizabeth Shewell West
(Mrs. Benjamin West)*
Matthew Pratt
Oil on canvas, circa 1765
76.2 x 63.5 cm. (30 x 25 in.)
The Pennsylvania Academy of the
Fine Arts, Philadelphia, Gift of
Mrs. Rosalie V. Tiers Jackson

School as a copy after West, and West's full-length of *Governor James Hamilton* [Figure 19] as an early work by Pratt which was "worthy to pass for one of West's."[5]

But Pratt's flesh colors, after he returned to America, were more delicate and muted than West's, and the effect is much softer. It seems that he may have learned more in England than what West had to teach. According to Charles Willson Peale, who arrived there in 1769, West heard that, after Pratt had left him, he had gone to Bristol to paint portraits and now imagined himself "much improved in his mode of colouring."[6] It may be that he looked carefully at the work of Thomas Gainsborough, who was painting nearby at Bath. Unfortunately no portraits have been traced to his Bristol period.[7]

A number of artists, about whom little is known, passed through West's studio in the late 1760s. This includes the Englishman, John Downman (circa

Figure 13.
The American School
Matthew Pratt
Oil on canvas, 1765
91.4 x 127.6 cm. (36 x 50¼ in.)
The Metropolitan Museum of Art, New York, Gift of Samuel P. Avery, 1897

Figure 14.
The Cricketers
Benjamin West
Oil on canvas, circa 1763
101.6 x 127 cm. (40 x 50 in.)
Private collection
Not in exhibition

Figure 15.
Pascal Paoli
Henry Benbridge
Oil on canvas, 1768
213.4 x 127 cm. (84 x 50 in.)
The Fine Arts Museums of
San Francisco, Gift of
Mr. and Mrs. John D. Rockefeller 3rd
Not in exhibition

1750-1824), who was there as a student from about 1768 to 1770 and maintained a close relationship afterwards with West. He gained recognition with his small portraits in chalk or oil and spoke of West as "my most beloved teacher."[8]

Henry Benbridge (1743-1812), a Philadelphia artist who visited Italy just after West had left, followed his predecessor to London, in late 1769, in order to gauge his own prospects there. He had previously sent from Italy a full-length portrait of the popular Corsican general, *Pascal Paoli* [Figure 15], to the exhibition at the Free Society of Artists, an earlier organization which was overshadowed by the more prestigious Royal Academy. He spent the winter in London and entered two portraits (both unlocated) in the Academy's spring exhibition before returning to America. West received him with kindness, and "insisted upon my eating at their house, & was very sorry they could not accommodate me with a room."[9] Although none of his London work is known, Benbridge presented himself as a mature artist rather than as a student. His style, which had been formed in Italy, remained remarkably consistent. Even his interest in the conversation piece probably originated in Rome. He seems to have regarded West as possible competition rather than as a source of inspiration.

Abraham Delanoy

Abraham Delanoy (1742-1795), from New York, arrived in London around 1766, according to Dunlap, and was "instructed for a short time" by West. While in the studio, he completed his only known London work, a likeness of West [Figure 16] dated 1766 on the reverse. The painting is distinctive in that it shows a peculiar consciousness of shape and a preoccupation with precise, linear definition, as in the way that the eyes, nose, lips, and jabot are circumscribed. The angular bend to the hair-ribbon makes it more attractive as a flat shape. These same tendencies, seen in his later American work, probably stemmed from his earlier style, of which nothing survives. In contrast to the portraits painted upon his return to New York—such as those of *Archibald Laidlie, D.D.* [Figure 17], or members of the Beekman family (all at the New-York Historical Society)—the *Benjamin West* is more painterly, with visible brushstrokes on the white cuffs and an attempt to manipulate light and shade to create a feeling of atmospheric volume which later, in his American work, was eliminated in favor of a tight and rigid linearity. As in Pratt's rendition of West, the modeling is still minimal. The drawn features are integrated less by color transitions than by a convincing display of foreshortening. Perhaps the only lasting lesson from London was that Delanoy learned to model at least the edges with subtle shadows. When Charles Willson Peale met him in London in 1767, he thought of Delanoy as an ungrateful and negligent student who showed a "want of respect" for West whom, in Peale's opinion, he should have seen daily. Delanoy did copy a picture by West which Dunlap describes as *Cupid Complaining to His Mother of a Sting from a Bee*, but which was probably the 1765 exhibited painting of *Venus and Cupid* (version not yet identified).[10] Nevertheless, the New Yorker's aesthetic outlook remained rooted in the colonial Dutch tradition of his native city, and his poses were invariably the stiff attitudes of about fifty years before.

West's supervision was certainly behind Delanoy's temporary adoption of a more sophisticated modeling. "In nature every thing is Round," was West's

Figure 16.
Benjamin West
Abraham Delanoy
Oil on canvas, 1766
61 x 50.8 cm. (24 x 20 in.)
The New-York Historical Society

outspoken view, "or at least Partakes the most of that forme which makes it imposeble that Nature, when seen in a light and shade, can ever appear liney."[11] He was replying to John Singleton Copley (1738-1815) in Boston, who had requested criticism of *Boy with a Squirrel* [Figure 18], a portrait that Copley had sent to the Society of Artists exhibition in 1766. West was especially concerned about teaching his students the effective uses of chiaroscuro. Years later, in 1785, he felt it necessary to tutor William Dunlap in this regard, and he incorporated this basic instruction in his discourse to the Royal Academy students in 1797, at which time he elaborated his demonstration to include color values as well.[12]

Both West and Reynolds (the first president of the Royal Academy) were surprised by Copley's great natural ability. Reynolds called his *Boy with a Squirrel* "a very wonderfull Performance" but criticized "a little Hardness in the

Figure 17.
Archibald Laidlie, D.D.
Abraham Delanoy
Oil on canvas, circa 1767
99 x 81.3 cm. (39 x 32 in.)
The New-York Historical Society

Drawing, Coldness in the Shades, An over minuteness," and, by implication, a lack of atmosphere.[13] Copley's dilemma was typical. The American colonial, prompted by the urge to paint, could hope to learn only through the use of prints, a possible apprenticeship or a few lessons, his observation of local artists (whose best work consisted almost wholly of portraits, the only kind of painting for which there was any demand in the Colonies), the very few European pictures in colonial collections, and what he could read about in the books which eulogized the Old Masters. Considered the best in Boston, Copley had no one from whom he could obtain rigorous criticism or against whom he could compare his progress. Naturally he felt insecure about how well his work would stand up against the finest in London.

Figure 18.
Boy With a Squirrel (Henry Pelham)
John Singleton Copley
Oil on canvas, 1765
76.8 x 63.5 cm. (30¼ x 25 in.)
Museum of Fine Arts, Boston,
Anonymous Gift
Not in exhibition

West praised his correctness of drawing and urged him to visit Europe, where he would have the opportunity to study great works of art "and feel from them what words Cannot Express. For this is a Source the want of which (I am sensible of) Cannot be had in America."[14] West's advice was sound. When Copley finally reached London in 1774, he went straight to him for counseling on his planned trip to the Continent. He respected West's experience, but he was never his student.

The American painter, far more than his counterpart abroad, had to depend upon the published word as the absolute authority in matters of art criticism. He could not have an opinion on Raphael other than what he had read. This gave printed descriptions an importance that they did not always have elsewhere. While West, as a child, read with delight of painters who were honoured by kings,[15] Copley's reading of the same passages made him deeply dissatisfied with

Boston: *Was it not for preserving the resembla[n]ce of perticular persons, painting would not be known in the plac[e]. The people generally regard it no more than any other usefull trade, as they sometimes term it, like that of a Carpenter tailor or shew maker, not as one of the most noble Arts in the World. Which is not a little Mortifying to me.*[16] One of the views fostered by Jonathan Richardson's *An Essay on the Theory of Painting* and Charles Alphonse Du Fresnoy's *The Art of Painting*, both read in the Colonies, was that the proper study of art was suitable for a gentleman because of its complexity. The history painter fulfilled a most exalted list of requirements, for he had an "Elevation of Genius" which included, aside from the talents of the finest painter, the qualities of a good historian and a good poet as well as a knowledge of anatomy, osteology, geometry, perspective, and architecture.[17] Even if there had been a demand for it, this left few aspirants. Copley, when he first visited London, was afraid that he would find composition, about which he had read, too difficult, and he was relieved to discover that it did not depend wholly upon imagination.[18] For the artist who wished to excel only in portraiture and who had the incentive to read about it, the obstacles were almost as great as those for the history painter: "To be a good face-painter, a degree of the historical, and poetical genius is requisite."[19] In general, if one wanted to rise above being a mere tradesman, to be able to justify an identification with the most famous names of the past, one had to study according to prescribed methods which assumed a knowledge of European art.

Sometimes the limner himself was not the first to realize the importance of European precedent. Instead, he was the compliant protégé of American patrons who made the decision to send him abroad in hopes that he would help to raise the cultural level of the community when he returned. This was the case with Charles Willson Peale (1741-1827) and his Maryland patrons.

Charles Willson Peale

As Peale stood on the doorstep with his letter of introduction, West was apparently in the midst of painting his full-length, or standing figure, of *Governor James Hamilton* [Figure 19] of Pennsylvania. The portrait dramatizes Hamilton, with a column and curtain behind, as a man of honor and importance who assumes a position of broad command with a sword against his side, one hand on his hip, and the other resting on a draped table. West needed someone to pose for the hand on the table, and Peale, coming in out of the February cold, was just the man. Thus, with an immediately binding experience, he became a student—the last of West's who could be considered a colleague in age, for he was only three years younger.

But what a difference in their careers! Peale, in 1767, had spent more of his life as a saddler and watchmaker than as a portrait painter. He was eager to learn from the seemingly sophisticated Benjamin West. Casting around for something for him to copy as a small watercolor, West lighted upon his *Elisha Raising the Shunammite's Son* [Figure 20], which he had set aside for the coming spring exhibition. Peale was soon able to report to his Maryland patron and friend, John Beale Bordley, that West had given him encouragement to pursue his career and had agreed to instruct him. He admired West's work, particularly the "luster & strength" of his coloring, more than that of his portrait-painting com-

Figure 19.
Governor James Hamilton
Benjamin West
Oil on canvas, 1767
241.2 x 155 cm. (95 x 61 in.)
Independence National Historical
Park, Philadelphia

petitors, Reynolds and Francis Cotes.[20]

Since Peale had an inclination to paint miniatures, West characteristically borrowed some examples from "the Best miniature Painter" (unidentified) he could find.[21] This broad-minded generosity was typical of West's treatment of his students, and, at various times in future years, he recommended that they go to another artist for advice in an area in which he did not specialize.

Peale, in his enterprising fashion, had already tried miniatures in Maryland, but chiefly his work had been in a larger size. It seems that he now turned to this form, because of its low-price salability, to help subsidize his stay in London. He painted them on the recommendation of a jeweler on Ludgate Hill who, by bringing Peale customers, and then by setting the likenesses so that they could be worn, added to his own business. Therefore, Peale's first effort was in the direction of miniatures, and he felt bold enough, after a year, to enter three in the 1768 annual exhibition of the Society of Artists. Of these only one has been located, the double portrait of John Beale Bordley's sons. Peale's large miniature

Figure 20.
Elisha Raising the Shunammite's Son
Benjamin West
Oil on canvas, 1765
100.6 x 127.6 cm. (40 x 50¼ in.)
The J. B. Speed Art Museum, Louisville

Figure 21.
Matthias and Thomas Bordley
Charles Willson Peale
Watercolor on ivory, 1767
9.2 x 10.8 cm. (3⅝ x 4¼ in.)
National Collection of Fine Arts,
Smithsonian Institution, Partial Gift of
Mr. and Mrs. Murray Lloyd
Goldsborough, Jr.

of *Matthias and Thomas Bordley* [Figure 21] shows the boys, as their father would have liked, dutifully improving themselves with the classical education for which they had been sent to England. As a miniature watercolor on ivory, now somewhat faded, it is an ambitious piece but basically a colored drawing by someone who has not totally mastered the technique. Outlining, as here, was always of prime importance to Peale. A good portrait meant a strong resemblance molded by convincing draftsmanship. Aesthetic considerations, such as color, atmosphere, and composition, were of much less importance in America than in England.

Peale and Delanoy are examples of West's students who were particularly receptive to what they wanted to learn, which was how to create a more perfect illusion of reality. They admired West's ability to convey three-dimensional form on a flat canvas. Peale's *Girl with a Toy Horse* [Figure 22], a full-length smaller than life (36 x 28 inches), exhibited in the same year as the miniatures, shows a new concern for establishing his subject in space. He has defined the background so that it recedes from the figure, which is now conscientiously shaded so that it occupies the room with a sculptural roundness which his earlier American

Figure 22.
Girl with a Toy Horse
Charles Willson Peale
Oil on canvas, 1768
91.4 x 71.1 cm. (36 x 28 in.)
The Bayou Bend Collection of
The Museum of Fine Arts, Houston

Figure 23.
Charles Willson Peale
Benjamin West
Oil on canvas, 1767/69
71.7 x 58.4 cm. (28¼ x 23 in.)
The New-York Historical Society,
Gift of Thomas J. Brejan

pictures did not have. The top of the girl's bodice clings to her shoulders and curves emphatically around them, while the arms are modeled as cylinders and the head is distinctly round. Spatial relationships are more carefully described than before; and, in a witty composition, Peale self-consciously duplicated the scene in the portrait over the mantelpiece so that there is a reduction of one image *ad infinitum*. At about this time, West painted a portrait of Peale [Figure 23], which has the same pale flesh color, almost ashen, and the chiaroscuro that became elements of Peale's style.

West did not charge for his advice, considering it the obligation of his position as well as a source of genuine enjoyment.[22] "He never, indeed, appeared to be more gratified," a contemporary observed, "than when engaged in enlightening the minds of those who looked up to him for instruction,"[23] treating them not as subordinates but as potential successors. The students that he took under his wing acted as apprentices, sometimes working on his canvases, as Peale apparently did,[24] and posing for the historical pictures. It seems that Peale was the only American student in 1769, when he visited West almost daily and posed for Regulus in *The Departure of Regulus* [Figure 24], West's first commission from the king. Thus Peale was the pupil who experienced the beginning of West's greatest success and would, of course, have joyously shared the responses of George III.

It was in late 1768 that the younger artist himself received a commission that was comparable in challenge to his adviser's work. Edmund Jenings, Bord-

Figure 24.
The Departure of Regulus
Benjamin West
Oil on canvas, 1769
224.8 x 304.8 cm. (88½ x 120 in.)
Her Majesty Queen Elizabeth II
Not in exhibition

ley's friend in London, engaged Peale to produce a full-length of that famous defender of American resistance to the Stamp Act, William Pitt, Lord Chatham. Jenings intended it as a gift for the courthouse of Westmoreland County, Virginia. However, since Pitt was too busy to pose, Peale was forced to resort to a statue of him in the guise of a Roman consul, which had been recently carved by Joseph Wilton. The portrait of *William Pitt* [Figure 25], as a togaed Roman orator, is an elaborate allegory of liberty centering on the message, applicable to Britain as well as to Rome, that "States which enjoy the highest Degree of Liberty are apt to be oppressive of those who are subordinate, and in Subjection to them"—such as America. To make the moral abundantly clear, it was spelled out in a published broadside describing the large mezzotint engraved after the picture. Peale was the author of the print as well. With his American orientation, he appreciated the value of interchangeable skills, and he planned to profit from selling the prints when he returned to Maryland.

Not only did he master the art of engraving outside of West's studio, but he experimented with modeling heads in clay and then casting them in plaster of Paris. West helped his friend by posing for a bust (unlocated), but he apparently did not teach him, since he did not work in clay himself. Peale seems again to have sought instruction elsewhere, and possibly, as has been suggested, from Joseph Wilton's assistant, a Mr. Capizoldi.[25]

Pursuing his diverse interests, Peale may have modeled from the Duke of Richmond's collection of antique casts at his house in Whitehall, which was open free of charge to interested artists, and he undoubtedly drew in the life class at the St. Martin's Lane Academy, a precursor of the Royal Academy's school. The surviving information on this institution, of which West was a director in 1766, is too meager for more than supposition, but it seems that Reynolds's students worked there as well.[26] The St. Martin's Lane Academy was such a recognized resource, closely associated with the exhibitions to which Peale contributed, that it would be natural for Peale—and even Pratt—to sketch from models in informal classes there.

Peale made further use of his opportunities by visiting Hampton Court nearby, where he could see Raphael's celebrated cartoons and some of the paintings in the Royal Collection. In London, there was also the Foundling Hospital, with a gallery of works donated by contemporary artists; public auction rooms with old pictures; and Benjamin West's growing collection of paintings and drawings by great masters, which was to become one of the finest private collections in the city. Other artists, such as Reynolds, collected on the side, and, in the normal course of visiting their studios, Peale would have learned something about quality and eclectic taste in collecting.

All this had a most humbling effect. Peale wrote, after his return to America, that he had no illusions about his ability: "What little I do is by mear imitation of what is before me. Perhaps I have a good eye, that is all, and not half the application that I now think is necessary." Reflecting the accepted belief of his day, he added with a tinge of regret: *A good painter of either portrait or History must be well acquainted with the Greesian and Roman Statues, to be able to draw them at pleasure by memory, and account for every beauty, must know the original cause of beauty in all he sees. These are some of the requisites of a good painter. These are more than I shall ever have time or opportunity to know.*[27] But West had reinforced in Peale's mind the value of working from nature. Peale was glad that he could "please" with his likenesses, while he left West

Figure 25.
William Pitt
Charles Willson Peale
Oil on canvas, probably 1768
238.8 x 144.8 cm. (94 x 57 in.)
Maryland Department of General
Services, Hall of Records and
Artistic Property Commissions

alone to reach for a higher plateau with his ennobling aim to instruct the public by examples of virtue.

Peale had not only acquired an improved technique but ideas which, when implemented, were of great benefit to fellow-Philadelphian artists. It was Peale, after all, who was in London at the time of the initial excitement over the establishment of the Royal Academy of Arts, and it was Peale who was so instrumental in the founding of a comparable institution, the Columbianum, in Philadelphia in 1795. Although short-lived, the Columbianum was the seed and the precedent for further such organizations in the United States; and its constitution (now in the American Philosophical Society, Philadelphia), providing for classes in drawing from casts and living models, a library, an annual exhibition of works by modern artists, and lectures by the president and professors of the academy, was very obviously taken from the regulations of the Royal Academy. Peale had also been so impressed with the value of displaying one's work that, throughout most of his subsequent career, he maintained a painting-room exhibition.

West's tendency to experiment and his desire to lead others of diverse persuasion saved him from adhering to a successful formula. His versatility is reflected in his collecting, which ranged widely among most of the well-known sixteenth- through eighteenth-century masters and eventually included a large number of works by artists as varied as Parmigianino, Rubens, Nicolas Poussin, the younger Teniers, and Aelbert Cuyp. During the 1770s, his own painting, particularly after he was appointed Historical Painter to the King in 1773, began to broaden into new areas. The famous *Death of General Wolfe* [Figure 1], exhibited in 1771, represented a departure from his usual classical subject matter and a switch to a larger size. It was followed, in the succeeding year, by the more exotic theme of *William Penn's Treaty with the Indians* (Pennsylvania Academy of the Fine Arts). Certainly he was emphasizing his unusual position as an American, but he was also showing his capacity for greater breadth. In his 1772 *Death of the Chevalier Bayard* [Figure 26], the figures lose their neoclassical clarity of definition and take on the blurred contours and richer colors of Rubens. His *Cave of Despair* [Figure 27], exhibited the next year, marks a further and more radical change in subject. Taken from Spenser's *Faerie Queene*, this scene shows Una restraining her Redcrosse Knight from stabbing himself under the spell of Despair's words. With a highly emotional scene, West indicated an interest in leading others into more sensational, even horrifying subjects, the kind that were beginning to be favored by his contemporary in London, Henry Fuseli. It was a timely display again of range. The kind of terror associated with violent death and the darkness of a cave fell within Edmund Burke's much-discussed category of the sublime in his seminal work of 1756, *Philosophical Inquiry into the Origins of Our Ideas of the Sublime and Beautiful*. West's brief forays, such as this one, helped maintain his position as London's foremost history painter.

Figure 26.
The Death of the Chevalier Bayard
Benjamin West
Oil on canvas, 1772
221 x 179.1 cm. (87¼ x 70½ in.)
Her Majesty Queen Elizabeth II
Not in exhibition

Figure 27.
Cave of Despair
Benjamin West
Oil on canvas, 1772
61 x 76 cm. (24 x 30 in.)
Yale Center for British Art,
New Haven,
Paul Mellon Collection

Joseph Wright

Little is known about his pupils in the 1770s. One of the most talented was the American, Joseph Wright (1756-1793), who journeyed to London in about 1773. He was preceded, in 1772, by an irrepressible and somewhat controversial mother who met, and quickly succeeded in alienating, George III with her anti-monarchical pronouncements. Patience Wright was a widow who supported her family, left behind in Philadelphia until she could establish herself by modeling likenesses in wax. Joseph Wright has the distinction of being the first American student to enter the Royal Academy schools. He was admitted in 1775, probably with West's help and on the basis of submitted drawings, and he was awarded a silver medal in 1778 for a bas-relief, probably in clay or wax, of an "Academy figure."[28] His mother had proudly written to Benjamin Franklin, the year before, that "my Son is a Exelent Portrait Painter Equal to mr West in taking likenesses."[29]

Dunlap, too, reported that Joseph became "a good portrait painter" before he left England in December of 1781, having even taken a likeness of the Prince of Wales,[30] but none of his London work is known to survive other than a self-caricature etching of about 1780 [Figure 28]. Like his mother, he seems to have had a feisty, patriotic spirit which is evident in the title of the etching—*Yankee-Doodle, or the American Satan.* Along the same lines, he exhibited a portrait of his mother (unlocated) at the Royal Academy in 1780, which was described as showing her modeling a head of Charles I, while looking at the nearby heads of King George and Queen Charlotte and obviously speculating on the possibilities of regicide. Even though the king was currently unpopular, the picture was

Figure 28.
Self-Portrait
Joseph Wright
Etching, circa 1780
17.2 x 13.3 cm. (6¾ x 5¼ in.)
The John Carter Brown Library,
Brown University, Providence

Figure 29.
Major Peter Labilliere
Henry Kingsbury,
after Joseph Wright
Engraving, 1780
28.6 x 20.3 cm. (11¼ x 8 in.)
The British Museum, London
Not in exhibition

provocative enough to raise some heated reactions. In the same year, Wright sent a *Portrait of a Gentleman* to the exhibition of the Society of Artists. Quite possibly this was the likeness of *Major Peter Labilliere*, an eccentric who once plotted to overthrow George III. Although the portrait is lost, a mezzotint after it [Figure 29], published late in 1780 by Henry Kingsbury, shows that it was, once again, a highly controversial piece with Labilliere seated before a number of petitions to the king.

50

We know something of Wright's political orientation during this period, but really nothing of how West influenced him, if at all. When it came time for Wright to leave, he went to West for a recommendation. Addressed to M. Pierre in Paris, professor at the French Royal Academy, West's introductory letter states Wright's intention to study in Paris and then go on to Rome for further improvement.[31] Since he never did visit the Papal City, possibly that idea was halfhearted and more West's than his. Wright's later portraits, with a relatively light palette and delicate modeling, appear closer to contemporary painting in France than in England. Recently an exceptionally fine full-length portrait by him, however, was discovered in Philadelphia, where it was probably painted about 1785; it is of special interest because of its dependence upon a specific English prototype. The pose in the portrait of *John Coats Browne* [Figure 30; color, page 125] is precisely that of Gainsborough's elegant *Blue Boy* [Figure 31]. The costume has been changed and a dramatic curtain and column added, as if this were a state portrait, but the plumed hat remains to help identify its source. Since *The Blue Boy* was not engraved until 1821, Wright must have copied it when he was in London.

Two other students overlapped at West's studio, but their aims separated

(left)
Figure 30.
John Coats Browne
Joseph Wright
Oil on canvas, circa 1785
156.8 x 109.9 cm. (61¾ x 43¼ in.)
The Fine Arts Museums of
San Francisco, Gift of Mr. and Mrs.
John D. Rockefeller 3rd

(right)
Figure 31.
The Blue Boy (Master John Buttall)
Thomas Gainsborough
Oil on canvas, 1770
177.8 x 121.9 cm. (70 x 48 in.)
Henry E. Huntington Library and
Art Gallery, San Marino, California
Not in exhibition

Gilbert Stuart

them almost at once: Gilbert Stuart and Ralph Earl. Although Stuart was four years younger, he was far more ambitious and impressionable; this, added to the fact that he became a member of West's household, makes him a particularly significant gauge of West's influence.

Stuart (1755-1828) did not immediately go to "the American Raphael." His purpose, on coming to London in 1775 from Newport, Rhode Island, was apparently to rejoin his old friend, Dr. Benjamin Waterhouse, to perfect himself in portrait painting, and to avoid the outbreak of war in America. In order to support himself at the beginning, he played a church organ, but he always had difficulty handling his finances and the salary of an organist was just not sufficient. Pride kept him at first from asking West's help. He painted his friend Waterhouse [Figure 32]—with whom he spent one day a week looking at pictures—with the simplified, blanket shadows reminiscent of the work of Copley. But this was for lack of other sitters. Finally, nearly penniless, Stuart sent a humble and rather awkward letter to West (in the collection of the New-York Historical Society). Beginning with "The Benevolence of your Disposition encourageth me," he gradually managed to stammer out his plea: "my hopes from home Blasted & incapable of returning thither, pitching headlong into misery I have this only hope I pray that it may not be too great to live & learn without being a Burthen, Should Mr West in his abundant kindness think of ought for me." Although the letter is undated, it must have been written not long before Stuart moved into West's house which, according to Stuart's daughter, was in the summer of 1777. Every week he was paid a half-guinea to paint draperies and finish West's portraits.[32] Occasionally he acted as a model, but he was also allowed to receive a few sitters in a separate studio and paint on his own. Thus an apprenticeship began that was to become unique among West's relationships with his students, because it developed into a partnership that was to last five years. West must have been particularly struck with Stuart's ability. By accepting a student in residence for several years, he went against a household rule that he had formed in about the year 1771.[33]

Stuart had ventured to exhibit a *Portrait of a Gentleman* (unlocated) in the Royal Academy spring exhibition of 1777, but he did not enter any work during his first year as West's pupil. Possibly, with his new opportunity, he now felt that he was not quite ready—that greater heights could be achieved. His next known work reveals a cocky self-consciousness as well as a new sophistication. It is his *Self-Portrait* [Figure 33] of 1778, which is remarkable for its unabashed identification with Rubens. Based on Rubens's *Self-Portrait* [Figure 34], which Stuart saw either in the Royal Collection or in an engraving,[34] this early demonstration of his skill apes even the signature on the Old Master's portrait: "G. Stuart Pictor / se ipso pinxit A. D. 1778 / Ætatis suae 24." Undoubtedly the precise wording was meant to be contrasted with Rubens's inscription, which ends "Ætatis suae xxxv." By choosing Rubens's pose and hat, Stuart was also following a precedent set in West's *Self-Portrait* of about 1770 [Figure 35]. Stuart's canvas shows that in the two years since his portrait of Waterhouse, he had learned to paint more freely and with much softer shadows, avoiding harsh contrasts.

These were years of experimentation. Although Stuart was not a student at the Royal Academy and therefore could not draw in their life class, he probably obtained permission through West to sketch the Academy's antique casts.[35] The importance of the casts was that they taught one how to idealize. Studies from life could be done in West's studio, but Stuart augmented his knowledge of anatomy by also attending lectures given, for a fee, to medical students by a Mr. Cruikshank.

The chance to live with West, then a thirty-nine-year-old court painter whose studio attracted the wealthy, was invaluable in itself. It meant mingling with fashionable society, people who fancied themselves as connoisseurs and, better yet, who actually bought pictures. It meant close observation of the winning ways of one of London's most successful artists. The contrast between Stuart's first incoherent, utterly abject letter and his later reputation for witty conversation suggests that the experience was not lost on him.

The major stylistic influences on Stuart's portraiture did not derive from West but rather from the simplified linearity of George Romney's portraits and the facile, decorative handling of paint in Gainsborough's work. Loose, rhythmi-

Figure 32.
Dr. Benjamin Waterhouse
Gilbert Stuart
Oil on canvas, circa 1776
55.9 x 45.7 cm. (22 x 18 in.)
Redwood Library and Athenaeum, Newport

Figure 33.
Self-Portrait
Gilbert Stuart
Oil on canvas, 1778
42.5 x 32.4 cm. (16¾ x 12¾ in.)
Redwood Library and Athenaeum,
Newport

cally visible brushwork, in the manner of Reynolds and Gainsborough, was high fashion. "If you wish to study portrait-painting," West once advised, "go to Sir Joshua,"[36] and this was probably similar to the counsel that he now gave Stuart.

Van Dyck was another source of inspiration, as he had been to Gainsborough. Stuart's portrait of *James Ward* [Figure 36], dated 1779, shows the engraver as a youth, with the pose and costume taken from Van Dyck. But it was an excuse for an experimental piece in which the young artist deliberately restricted himself to a harmony of three basic colors—pale blue, chestnut, and white—enriched by surface glazing in the manner of both Gainsborough and Van Dyck. Ward's shoulder, for instance, is painted with a partially impasted white, overlaid with transparent pink and blue washes, so that the result has an opalescent richness. Very noticeable, too, is Stuart's new adoption of the sketchy brushwork so admired by contemporaries.

Gainsborough's influence is also reflected in Stuart's early attempt at a full-length, *Henrietta Elizabeth Frederica Vane* [Figure 37; color, page 126], which was perhaps in the exhibition of the Incorporated Society of Artists in 1783. With

Figure 34.
Self-Portrait
Peter Paul Rubens
Oil on canvas
85.8 x 61.6 cm. (33¾ x 24½ in.)
Her Majesty Queen Elizabeth II
Not in exhibition

a delicate palette and a nervous line, akin to Gainsborough's, Stuart constructed as stylish a portrait as possible, following the English tradition of an outdoor pose where the figure is flanked by autumnal foliage and a fading sunset. He revealed his inexperience, however, in the rather tentative stance: the position of the feet, even if she is leaning against a support, is disturbingly uncertain. The artist, as he himself realized, was best at half-length portraits which showed the subject seated and visible to the waist or perhaps just below the knee. The only time Stuart ever really excelled in a full, standing figure was in his portrait of William Grant as *The Skater*, very possibly his first trial in this scale.

The Skater [Figure 38] captured the public's interest and received high praise when it was entered in the Royal Academy exhibition of 1782. With arms folded and an intent expression on his face, Grant is represented in the attitude of ice-skating on the Serpentine against the wintry backdrop of Hyde Park. The theme was suggested to Stuart when he started to paint Grant in his studio on a day which was so chilly that Grant complained that it would be better to spend one's time skating. The finished work, so novel in conception, was one of the most popular contributions to the Royal Academy's annual show. At a time

Figure 35.
Self-Portrait
Benjamin West
Oil on canvas, circa 1770
76.8 x 64.4 cm. (30¼ x 25⅜ in.)
National Gallery of Art,
Washington, D.C.,
Andrew Mellon Collection, 1942

Figure 36.
James Ward
Gilbert Stuart
Oil on canvas, 1779
74.9 x 63.5 cm. (29½ x 25 in.)
The Minneapolis Institute of Arts,
the William Hood Dunwoody Fund

when not many pictures were specifically mentioned, the reviewer for the *Morning Chronicle* called it "animated and well drawn."[37]

"Stuart seldom fails of a likeness," the critic for the *St. James's Chronicle* observed, "but wants freedom of pencil and elegance of taste." The twenty-seven-year-old artist was rapidly acquiring both, and to such an extent that most of his contemporaries in the art world would probably have challenged this criticism. While other newspaper comments were generally not very revealing, this same reviewer added the only evidence we have of a special arrangement between Stuart and his instructor: "Mr. Stuart is in partnership with Mr. West." Applicants for portraits were told "by Mr. West that Mr. Stuart is the only portrait painter in the world; and by Mr. Stuart that no man has any pretensions in history but Mr. West."[38] Stuart assisted West in his studio and supervised the other students. When not busy, he sometimes would fence with them with mahlsticks, or, in West's absence, go through his imitation of "the American Raphael" at work. It was not a business partnership so much as a friendship based upon mutual respect.

Figure 37.
Henrietta Elizabeth Frederica Vane
Gilbert Stuart
Oil on canvas, 1782–83
167.4 x 98.1 cm. (65⅞ x 38⅝ in.)
Smith College Museum of Art,
Northampton, Massachusetts,
Given in memory of Jessie Rand
Goldthwait ('90) by her husband
and daughter, 1957

After the 1782 exhibition, Stuart's increased reputation was an incentive to set out on his own. It would have been foolish not to take the hint of a veteran artist, Nathaniel Dance, who told him: "You are strong enough to stand alone . . . those who would be unwilling to sit to Mr. West's pupil, will be glad to sit to Mr. Stuart."[39] Of course he was right. Unlike most of West's students, who hurried back to America, Stuart stayed on in London for five years and established himself as one of the city's most fashionable portraitists. He found the English training congenial to his own nature and, under West's liberal guidance, he blossomed to full potential. The experience was as vital to his artistic development as it was the reverse to Ralph Earl. It brought out just those latent qualities in him which later made him West's most celebrated student. Unlike Earl, he was able to compete successfully, on their own terms, with Romney and Reynolds. He achieved not just a strong resemblance but a picture which derived aesthetic merit from a decorative distribution of color and paint texture. Stuart forged a likeness out of short, jabbing strokes and fresh, transparent tints with a spontaneity that seemed remarkably clever; and his concern for overall beauty of effect gave a certain dignifying elegance to even a plain sitter.

Figure 38.
The Skater (William Grant)
Gilbert Stuart
Oil on canvas, 1782
245 x 147.6 cm. (96⅝ x 58⅛ in.)
National Gallery of Art,
Washington, D.C.,
Andrew W. Mellon Collection
Not in exhibition

Figure 39.
Mary Ann Carpenter
Ralph Earl
Oil on canvas, 1779
120 x 88.9 cm. (47¼ x 35 in.)
Worcester Art Museum

Ralph Earl

Ralph Earl (1751-1801), on the other hand, was less interested in technical finesse. He placed his priorities on a simplified but convincing representation of the sitter and the background. At best, his works have a kind of raw power, a force of characterization that recalls Copley's American portraits. Since Earl apparently admired Copley most of all, the English artists had less to teach him. His style went through a period of adjustment in London, but he lost most of what he had learned after returning to America.

As his early biographer, Dunlap, noted, Earl painted in the Colonies in 1777 "as Earle thought, in the manner of Copley." Two full-lengths, of the Rev. and

Mrs. Timothy Dwight (both unlocated), from that year "showed some talent, but the shadows were black as charcoal or ink."[40] He was enterprising, however. We know that he left his studio in New Haven, Connecticut, in the summer of 1775 in order to sketch four scenes of Concord and Lexington with the introduction of imaginary soldiers to simulate the recent battles. His traveling companion, Amos Doolittle, made engravings from the pictures which were advertised as "engraven on Copper, from original paintings taken on the spot."[41] Nevertheless, it was not his ingenuity that brought him to London in 1778, but rather his desire to escape imprisonment as a Loyalist spy. He had been disinherited by his father and expelled from Connecticut for what appeared to be treachery, having furnished the British at least once with intelligence information.

Earl's first known English portraits, signed and dated 1779, are of *Mary Ann Carpenter* [Figure 39], and her brother *William* (Worcester Art Museum). The Carpenter family, from Aldeby Priory near Norwich, Norfolk, were undoubtedly introduced to Earl by Captain John Money, who had helped Earl escape from the American coast and who happened to live near Norwich. At first, Earl may well have intended to establish himself as a painter in Norfolk. He had little money, since there was not much hope that he would receive what he had requested for Loyalist compensation from the Lord Commissioners of the Treasury, and in Norfolk he could avoid the competition of London.

Earl's precise connection with West is still unclear. Dunlap, a contemporary who admittedly was not always reliable about dates, believed that Earl studied under "the direction of Mr. West, immediately after the independence of his country was established" (September of 1783). More recent authors take a different view and maintain that Earl probably went to West almost at once.[42] The evidence, purely visual, shows that Earl's 1779 portraits of the Carpenters are not inconsistent with his American work as represented by the one surviving portrait—that of *Roger Sherman* [Figure 40]—and could have been painted without any interaction with English art. On the other hand, Earl's next dated portrait, after a gap of three years, the 1782 *Mrs. John Johnston* [Figure 41], is more technically advanced. With greater and more subtle modeling, freer brushwork, and a more relaxed pose, this portrait stems from Earl's English contemporaries. At the same time, he had by now learned to rely less on his sitter and more on his imagination. Earlier, his hands, for instance, were individualized. They were portraits of hands; but here they are the characterless, conventional forms that are usual in English pictures. These changes could have occurred with or without West's influence, since, as we have seen, his presence did not necessarily mean the imposition of his style.

Copley continued to be a source of inspiration. When Earl ventured to enter his *Colonel George Onslow* [Figure 42] in his first Royal Academy exhibition of 1783, *The Morning Post, and Daily Advertiser* singled it out as "A most excellent likeness" with "parts of the drapery remarkably well cast."[43] Although an uneven painter, Earl, like Copley, was interested in *trompe-l'oeil* effects. This is particularly evident in his realistic representation of material in *Onslow*; in

Figure 40.
Roger Sherman
Ralph Earl
Oil on canvas, date unknown
164.1 x 26.4 cm. (64⅝ x 49¾ in.)
Yale University Art Gallery,
New Haven,
Gift of Roger Sherman White
Not in exhibition

the projecting paper in *A Master in Chancery Entering the House of Lords* (1783; Smith College Museum of Art), exhibited in 1784; or in the inkstand, carefully highlighted, in his 1783 *Lady Williams and Child* (Metropolitan Museum of Art). Making fun of his inability to compete with Copley, Earl would say of a just-completed picture: "I entend to offer it to Copely to coppey for his enprovement."[44]

He was writing, at this moment, on September 23, 1784, from Windsor, where he was visiting West and possibly painting under his supervision. Periodically, the Historical Painter to the King moved to his second studio in Wind-

Figure 41.
Mrs. John Johnston
Ralph Earl
Oil on canvas, 1782
76.8 x 64.2 cm. (30¼ x 25¼ in.)
Parker Soren, great-great-great grandson of the subject
Not in exhibition

sor Castle to work on his many royal commissions, which now centered on a series of vast canvases to illustrate Biblical instances of revealed religion. Here then, in 1784, was the first proof of West's instruction.

The recipient of Earl's letter was a young apothecary-doctor, Joseph Trumbull, from Massachusetts, whom Earl painted in this same year. The portrait of *Joseph Trumbull* [Figure 43] is perhaps Earl's closest approximation to the style of the English artist George Romney. Earl was expanding and, like Stuart, he was more attracted to Romney's thinly painted heads, with fresh colors, minimal shading, and simple outlines, than to the multilayered technique of Reynolds. Nonetheless, Reynolds encouraged the kind of flamboyant brushwork that appears on Trumbull's waistcoat, which was now almost universal among the London artists. This indulgence in paint texture, as in the white, impasted jabot, was new

Figure 42.
Colonel George Onslow, M.P.
Ralph Earl
Oil on canvas, 1783
132.1 x 106.7 cm. (52 x 42 in.)
Mrs. Ralph Earle
Not in exhibition

to Earl and came gradually. As always, he was interested in the careful depiction of costume, or "stuffs," such as in the coat edge. This detail was as important as the transparency of the gauze-like bodice in his 1784 portrait of his English wife, *Ann Whiteside* [Figure 44]. He had acquired the English manner: greater facility, softer modeling, a less linear approach.

Earl tried larger, more ambitious pictures as well. With an irreverence which seems to have been typical, he produced, at some time in England, a *Reclining Hunter* [Figure 45], which pokes fun at the gentleman-hunter, very likely a Londoner. He settles under a tree with a supercilious grin, having shot everything in sight. His latest rampage has brought down a curious collection of birds, a donkey, and even a cow. Making the most of his holiday, he has stuffed his tricorn hat with as many mushrooms as he could pick—and has thus proved his

Figure 43.
Joseph Trumbull
Ralph Earl
Oil on canvas, 1784
76.5 x 63.5 cm. (30 1/8 x 25 in.)
Historic Deerfield, Inc., Massachusetts
Not in exhibition

all-round prowess in the woods. Probably done about 1784, the background has overtones of Gainsborough, in the sketchy foliage against a pink sky; and Earl has tried an English glazing technique in the blue coat. But such experimentation did not last. After Earl returned to America in 1785, he executed some of his finest portraits with the same pre-London emphasis on character rather than technique or exact anatomical accuracy. At times they were turned out almost as a formula in treatment and pose. He drew sporadically upon his English experience, at first for a more liquid use of paint, more sophisticated highlighting, and some ideas for poses and more complicated backgrounds. But he never learned to subordinate background props to the figure, and thus he ignored the "cry of the English

Figure 44.
Ann Whiteside (Mrs. Ralph Earl)
Ralph Earl
Oil on canvas, 1784
118.3 x 96 cm. (46⅜ x 37⅞ in.)
Amherst College, Mead Art Museum,
Massachusetts

School" which was unforgettable to Stuart: "sink your drapery . . . & bring out the flesh."[45] Earl's American backdrops tend to compete with the sitters in a way that separated him from the taste of London.

In July of 1774 West shifted his London residence to a new site, on which he had built with borrowed money. It became the well-known No. 14, Newman Street, a spacious house with three exhibition galleries and workshops large enough to accommodate the royal commissions. When he first entered West's house in 1784, Dunlap, at age eighteen, was nearly overwhelmed by "the long gallery leading from the dwelling-house" to the studio at the rear.[46] The best description, however, is still Leigh Hunt's, made from his recollection of visits in the 1790s: *The gallery was a continuation of the house-passage, and, together with*

66

one of those rooms and the parlor, formed three sides of a garden, very small but elegant, with a grass-plot in the middle, and busts upon stands under an arcade. The gallery . . . was hung with the artist's sketches all the way. At the back there were two "lofty rooms" which "contained the largest of West's pictures; and in the farther one, after stepping softly down the gallery, as if reverencing the dumb life on the walls, you generally found the mild and quiet artist at his work."[47]

Another visitor, a tourist from Germany, jotted down her impressions in a 1786 diary. She was making the rounds of favored studios and had been to see those of Reynolds and Gainsborough before finding her way to Newman Street: *We found West, the painter of historical scenes, there in person, surrounded by pupils and masterpieces by his own hand. He received us nobly, though unassumingly, in the manner of all great achievement. He works in a room lit from above, and the gallery leading to it is hung with sketches of completed pictures of which engravings had been made. He showed us some of the large historical canvases he is painting. . . . Then he led us to his collection of old and modern*

Figure 45.
Reclining Hunter
Ralph Earl
Oil on canvas, circa 1784
115.5 x 151.1 cm. (45½ x 59½ in.)
Sabin Galleries, London

WEST'S PICTURE GALLERY,
NEWMAN ST LONDON.

Figure 46.
West's Picture Gallery
John Le Keux, after Cattermole
Engraving, 1821
12.7 x 17.8 cm. (5 x 7 in.)
The British Museum, London
Not in exhibition

masters, for he possesses one choice piece by every famous painter. From here, probably at the suggestion of West, the diarist went on to Stuart's house, where she found that "he, too, lives as if in the hall of the temple of the Muses, in rooms of magnificent style," in emulation of the most respected artists.[48]

But West's "establishment" became the most impressive of all. In the early nineteenth century, the canvases in his one-man museum were dramatically draped, with special light effects, and some of them were even roped off behind a dais. John Sartain, an American engraver, recalled seeing West's huge *Death on a Pale Horse* and *Christ Rejected* in the Newman Street gallery [Figure 46] after West's death: *A canopy resting on slender pillars stood in the middle of the room, its opaque roof concealing the skylight from the spectator, who stood thus in a sort of half-obscure dimness, while both pictures received the full flood of light. The effect was very fine and at that time novel.*[49] Very probably this is a description of the gallery after West's sons fitted it up in 1821 as an admission-charging museum, but the presence of the living master at the height of his reputation would have made it awesome enough during his lifetime.

West's first-generation students, on the whole, were portrait painters interested in improving themselves in just such ways that would win greater approval in the Colonies, where the fashion in portraiture was set by England but where the standards were somewhat different. As Stuart complained after his return to America, many years later, "In England my efforts were compared to those of Vandyke, Titian and other great painters—but here! they compared them to the works of the Almighty!"[50] With such an emphasis at home on realistic portrayal, learning the techniques of illusion was the highest priority for those students who went abroad.

Notes

1. West had also been "intimate" with James Claypoole, Jr., Pratt's first cousin and fellow-apprentice under Claypoole, Sr. Claypoole, Jr., later intended to visit West in London. See John Sartain, *The Reminiscences of a Very Old Man, 1808-1897* (New York: 1969) reprint ed., p. 148.

2. William Sawitzky, *Matthew Pratt, 1734-1805* (New York: 1942), p. 19.

3. John W. Jordan, "The Fellowship Fire Company of Philadelphia, Organized 1738," *The Pennsylvania Magazine of History and Biography* 27, no. 4 (1903): p. 479.

4. John Wilmerding, *American Art* (New York: 1976), p. 47 mentions the current state of this problem of identification and concludes, for different reasons, that the figure at the easel is not Pratt.

5. Cf. Dunlap, *History*, vol. 1, p. 101. The full-length of Hamilton that Sully mentioned seeing at Woodlands must be the one by West. There is no further evidence that Pratt ever painted such a full-length.

6. Sartrain, *Reminiscences*, p. 148.

7. His later portrait, of apparently 1773, of *Mary Jemina Balfour*, at the Virginia Historical Society, suggests knowledge of Gainsborough's use of glazes but also appears to be puzzlingly unique in Pratt's *oeuvre*.

8. Dr. [George Charles] Williamson, *John Downman, A.R.A.* (London: 1907), p. xii.

9. Robert G. Stewart, *Henry Benbridge (1743-1812): American Portrait Painter* (Washington, D.C.: 1971), p. 18.

10. Letter (copy), C. W. Peale to Rembrandt Peale, October 28, 1812, vol. 12, C. W. Peale's Letter Book, American Philosophical Society, Philadelphia; Dunlap, *History*, vol. 1, p. 161.

11. Guernsey Jones, ed., *Letters and Papers of John Singleton Copley and Henry Pelham, 1739-1776* (New York: 1970), reprint ed., p. 44.

12. Dunlap, *History*, vol. 1, p. 259; Galt, *Life of Benjamin West*, pt. 2, pp. 111-13.

13. Jones, *Copley and Pelham*, pp. 41-42.

14. Jules D. Prown, *John Singleton Copley* (Cambridge, Mass.: 1966), vol. 1, p. 51.

15. Galt, *Life of Benjamin West*, pt. 1, pp. 29-30. Also see Jonathan Richardson, *Theory of Painting*, p. 32.

16. Jones, *Copley and Pelham*, pp. 65-66.

17. J. Richardson, *Theory of Painting*, p. 21; Du Fresnoy, *The Art of Painting*, pp. 71-72.

18. Prown, *Copley*, vol. 2, p. 245.

19. J. Richardson, *Theory of Painting*, p. 21, and Robert R. Wark, ed., *Sir Joshua Reynolds: Discourses on Art* (San Marino, Calif.: 1959), p. 72 (Reynolds's Fourth Discourse, 1771). This idea was long in dying. Cf. Galt, *Life of Benjamin West*, vol. 2, p. 94, where it appears in West's second discourse; and R. Ackermann, *The Microcosm of London* (London: 1808), vol. 1, p. 4.

20. Charles Coleman Sellers, *Charles Willson Peale* (New York: 1969), p. 57.

21. *Ibid.*

22. "Benjamin West, Esq., President of the Royal Academy," in *La Belle Assemblée* (London: 1808), vol. 4, no. 2, p. 52.

23. Dunlap, *History*, vol. 1, p. 94.

24. Sellers, *C. W. Peale*, p. 56.

25. *Ibid.*, p. 65.

26. Robert C. Alberts, *Benjamin West: A Biography* (Boston: 1978), p. 72; William T. Whitley, *Artists and Their Friends in England, 1700-1799* (New York: 1968) reprint ed., vol. 1, p. 150.

27. Sellers, *C. W. Peale*, p. 104.

28. "Students admitted in the Royal Academy from 1769 to 1827," Library of the Royal Academy, London; supplemented by letter of July 10, 1978, to the author from Constance-Anne Parker, Librarian of the Royal Academy. This is the source for all further mention of enrollments at the Royal Academy.

29. Charles Coleman Sellers, *Patience Wright, American Artist and Spy in George III's London* (Middletown, Conn.: 1976), p. 108.

30. Dunlap, *History*, vol. 1, p. 312.

31. Letter, B. West to M. Pierre, Dec. 7, 1781, Dreer Collection, Historical Society of Pennsylvania, Philadelphia.

32. Morgan, *Gilbert Stuart*, p. 4.

33. Jones, *Copley and Pelham*, p. 118.

34. Possibly the frontispiece to J.F.M. Michel, *Histoire de la Vie de P.P. Rubens* (Brussels: 1771).

35. William T. Whitley, *Gilbert Stuart* (Cambridge, Mass.: 1932), p. 19.

36. Dunlap, *History*, vol. 1, p. 185.

37. Whitley, *Stuart*, p. 32.

38. *Ibid.*, p. 30.

39. Dunlap, *History*, vol. 1, p. 180.

40. *Ibid.*, p. 223.

41. Laurence B. Goodrich, *Ralph Earl, Recorder for an Era* (New York: 1967), p. 3.

42. William and Susan Sawitzky, "Two Letters from Ralph Earl with Notes on his English Period," *Worcester Art Museum, Annual Report for the Year 1960* (Worcester, Mass.: 1961), vol. 8, p. 19; Goodrich, *Ralph Earl*, p. 6; Harold Spencer, *The American Earls: Ralph Earl, James Earl, R.E.W. Earl*, The William Benton Museum of Art (Storrs, Conn.: 1972), p. 4.

43. Goodrich, *Ralph Earl*, p. 20.

44. Letter, Ralph Earl to Joseph Trumbull, September 23, 1784, Deerfield Academy, Deerfield, Massachusetts.

45. Morgan, *Gilbert Stuart*, p. 82.

46. Dunlap, *History*, vol. 1, p. 67.

47. Leigh Hunt, *The Autobiography of Leigh Hunt, with Reminiscences of Friends and Contemporaries* (New York: 1965), vol. 1, p. 100.

48. Sophie von La Roche, *Sophie in London, 1786*, tr. Clare Williams (London: 1933), pp. 152-53.

49. Sartain, *Reminiscences*, p. 169.

50. "American Painters," *American Quarterly Review*, 17, no. 33 (March 1835): p. 177.

THE SECOND GENERATION
1780-1800

More than any other generation, this one at the Newman Street studio belonged to Benjamin West. "His virtues and his talents have shed a lustre around his name" was the way their spokesman, William Dunlap, regarded the instructor, "and we view him by a light radiating from himself."[1] The agreeable Mrs. West, who was so happily married that she could find no fault with her husband, called these younger men her "adopted sons."[2] Her real sons and only children, Raphael and Benjamin, Jr., both lazy but possessed of some artistic talent, were old enough to take their places as members of this, the generation of West's first history painters.

Although portrait limners continued to come to him, West found his spiritual heirs in the historical artists. The first was John Trumbull (1756-1843), the aristocratic son of the governor of Connecticut. As Dunlap put it, he was "emphatically well-born."[3] Educated at Harvard, he was an officer in the Continental Army and an aide-de-camp to General Washington before he resigned his commission in 1777 to become a painter. His plan was to study under John Singleton Copley in Boston but, when he arrived there, he found that Copley had already gone to England. There seemed to be one recourse left. He rented what had been John Smibert's studio, which still contained copies after Old Master pictures. By imitating these paintings, only once removed from the masterpieces themselves, he set out to teach himself, for "there remained in Boston no artist from whom I could gain oral instruction."[4]

He was tempted to make the voyage to England, but there was reason to hesitate. The war was still in progress, and he could easily be arrested on the streets of London because of his reputation as a rebel. Finally the assurance came from a friend in England that, if he pursued a career in art alone, no notice would be taken of his past. As it turned out, Trumbull was arrested as a spy in 1780, after about three months with West, and placed under guard for about seven months before being deported. He had been caught carrying letters with ambiguous references, still not clear, which seem to indicate that he was involved in some intrigue against the British war effort.

Although his first period with West was brief, Trumbull received encouragement and was able to work from copies (unlocated) of Raphael's *Madonna of the*

John Trumbull

Chair and Correggio's *St. Jerome*. More ambitiously, he did a small full-length, from memory, of *George Washington* [Figure 47]. It appears to have been influenced by an earlier, 1778 half-length copy (now cut down; Yale University Art Gallery) that Trumbull painted in Boston from Charles Willson Peale's 1776 life portrait (The Brooklyn Museum). The 1778 portrait apparently later belonged to West.[5] In any case, the resulting full-length is much more freely executed and painted with a lighter palette than Trumbull's earlier likenesses, such as the 1778 portrait of his brother, *Joseph Trumbull* [Figure 48], which, although strongly

Figure 47.
George Washington
John Trumbull
Oil on canvas, 1780
91.4 x 71.1 cm. (36 x 28 in.)
The Metropolitan Museum of Art,
New York, Bequest of
Charles Allen Munn, 1924

Figure 48.
Joseph Trumbull
John Trumbull
Oil on canvas, 1778
130.8 x 101.6 cm. (51½ x 40 in.)
The Connecticut Historical Society,
Hartford, on indefinite loan
from the Pilgrim Society

reminiscent of Copley, is very emphatically drawn and then cloaked in dark shadows. Washington, as a subject, had already captured the public's curiosity, so it was not difficult to find a buyer for the portrait in M. de Neufville, a banker from Amsterdam, who evidently agreed to have the picture published by Valentine Green as an engraving.

Trumbull continued his studies in Bridewell Prison. Completing his copy in oils of the *St. Jerome*, he went on to do the best he could with chalk drawings. One of his visitors was Stuart, who could not resist painting him as "Bridewell Jack" [Figure 49]. Trumbull added the body, the background, and the window bars.

Figure 49.
John Trumbull
Gilbert Stuart (and John Trumbull)
Oil on canvas, 1781
76.2 x 63.5 cm. (30 x 25 in.)
Pilgrim Hall, Plymouth, Massachusetts

Mather Brown

While Trumbull was in jail, Mather Brown (1761-1831) arrived in April of 1781. Young, impressionable, and talented, this artist was from Boston, where he and Trumbull had been friends. He reached London by way of Paris, where he received a letter of recommendation to West from Benjamin Franklin. Having had some lessons in Boston, about six years before, from Gilbert Stuart, he intended to reside "sometime in London," as a contemporary expressed it, "with a View of perfectioning himself in the Art of Miniature painting."[6]

Fortunately, some of Brown's correspondence survives. His first letter to his Boston relatives, after more than four months in London, reassured them that he was practicing "gratis" with the famous Mr. West, "who affords me every Encouragement."[7] He drew from the antique casts in the Royal Academy, and, on the basis of these sketches, was admitted into the school on January 7, 1782, thus becoming the second American, after Joseph Wright, to take full advantage of this opportunity, for which there was no charge.

Within about a month, Brown was judged qualified to join the class that met in the evening with a live model. The students chose seats by lot and adjusted their candles while the Visitor, or rotating supervisor who was appointed for a month, set the pose. They then drew, rather than painted, from the nude model for about two hours, from six to eight o'clock. Alternatively, the students could draw from the plaster casts. The models were changed twice a week, and, since Brown had just had his twentieth birthday, he could sketch from a female model as well. The purpose of this drawing exercise was to learn greater hand control, accuracy of observation, and skill in modeling with the soft shadows provided by candlelight. After the sketching session, Brown reported that he attended lectures on anatomy and perspective.[8]

Aside from these classes, Mather Brown may have listened to James Barry, who, as professor of painting, gave a series of lectures which dealt with theory and, most particularly, the importance of history painting. Then there were discourses given biennially by the president of the Royal Academy, Sir Joshua Reynolds. These were published and, although somewhat contradictory and eclectic in approach, became the lasting embodiment of English neoclassical theory. Consistent with the ethos of his period, Reynolds urged the artist to endeavor to improve mankind with "the grandeur of his ideas." Although Reynolds warned that "Nature . . . is not to be too closely copied," Stuart saw this piece of advice as Reynolds's flaw, for there was "more poetry than truth" in the president's work.[9] Brown's opinions were, finally, most influenced by those expressed in West's studio, where he learned how to manage color and composition and how to interpret what he heard at the Academy. It was generally understood there that the student would receive his practical training in the use of oil paints by establishing himself as either a protégé or an apprentice of some outside master.

"While I dayly overlook Mr. West in producing those Miracles of Historic Art," Brown wrote home, "I seem to feel more than Inspiration."[10] West believed that a student "must be stimulated and encouraged . . . he must feel his profession not only honorable, but something more in its perfection than is common to mankind."[11] Brown abandoned his miniature portraits in 1782 and, with the initial zeal of a convert, made a few attempts at history painting (unlocated); but he was not yet ready.[12]

The earliest life-size portrait that can be attributed to him with certainty is a full-length *Girl at a Harpsichord* [Figure 50], which probably dates from about 1782. There is a simplicity here, with delicate colors, as well as a subtle accuracy that one might expect in a miniature painter. It is clearly a student work, with a kind of localized, amateurish modeling which tends to separate features rather than unify the head. But he was learning rapidly. The background has the blue hills and romantic sunset which were commonplace in English portraiture, while the pool of fading sunlight on the classical staircase is a slightly more sophisticated touch.

Figure 50.
Girl at a Harpsichord
Mather Brown
Oil on canvas, circa 1782
127 x 101.6 cm. (50 x 40 in.)
Glasgow Art Gallery and Museum

Brown's enthusiasm was so fired that he entered a *Portrait of a Gentleman* (unlocated) in the 1782 Royal Academy exhibition, only a year after he had arrived. *The London Courant*, of May 8, 1782, actually mentioned it and called it "a medium performance," which was favorable, considering the criticism of others. His portrait style was coming under the influence of Gilbert Stuart, who had not yet left West and was the chief portrait painter in the Newman Street studio. Just as Trumbull had submitted his work to Stuart for criticism,[13] Brown was also apparently placed under his guidance.

Gilbert Stuart had an independent mind, and his advice did not always coincide with that of the master. For instance, he did not approve of the opaque flesh colors that West used in such portraits as *The Drummond Family* [Figure 51].

When he revisited the Newman Street studio in about 1785, he complained to one of the students there: *When Benny teaches the boys, he says, "yellow and white there," and he makes a streak, "red and white there," another streak, "blue-black and white there," another streak, "brown and red there, for a warm shadow," another streak, "red and yellow there," another streak. But Nature does not colour in streaks. Look at my hand; see how the colours are mottled and mingled, yet all is clear as silver.*[14] In West's studio, in the master's absence, Stuart used to speak freely of his own superiority as a portrait-painter, adding impishly, "No man ever painted history if he could obtain employment in portraits;"[15] but he never forgot the indebtedness of all of them to the indulgence of a certain history painter.

Brown's portraits, such as the one *Frederick W. Geyer* [Figure 52], a Boston Loyalist, come remarkably close to Stuart's contemporary work. There is

Figure 51.
The Drummond Family
Benjamin West
Oil on canvas, 1781
152.4 x 129.5 cm. (60 x 51 in.)
IBM Corporation, Armonk, New York

Figure 52.
Frederick W. Geyer
Mather Brown
Oil on canvas, 1784
76.2 x 63.5 cm. (30 x 25 in.)
Dr. and Mrs. Henry C. Landon, III

the same emphasis on fresh color and an effect of spontaneity which decorates but does not interfere with the essential strength of the likeness. Brown became more flamboyant than Stuart, with wilder and longer brushstrokes and, frequently, more romantic attitudes, as in his full-length *Portrait of a Gentleman* [Figure 53] from probably the late 1780s. As one young American characterized Brown's style, "You will find it very rough, but that is the modish stile of painting, introduced by Sir Joshua Reynolds."[16]

Around the year 1785, after Stuart and Brown had both left West's studio (Stuart in 1782 and Brown, without an abrupt end, sometime afterwards), a certain amount of rivalry developed between them. Far more established in his career, Stuart won the lucrative commission from publisher John Boydell to complete fifteen portraits of contemporary artists who had worked on the illustrations for Boydell's edition of Shakespeare. His likeness of *William Woollett* [Figure

Figure 53.
Portrait of a Gentleman
Mather Brown
Oil on canvas, late 1780s
224.8 x 137.2 cm. (88½ x 54 in.)
The Beaverbrook Canadian
Foundation, Beaverbrook Art Gallery,
Fredericton, N.B., Canada

54], the man who produced the famous engraving of West's *Death of Wolfe*, was one of this group. The format, a half-length view of a seated figure, here enriched with the contrasting reds of a dressing-gown and turban, was to become practically a formula for Stuart.

Brown's competitive status, on the other hand, was confirmed by the decided preference of Thomas Jefferson, a discerning connoisseur, who was then serving as the American Ambassador to France. Jefferson commissioned a portrait of himself (unlocated) in 1786, which was considered such a striking resemblance that John Adams, then the American Ambassador to England, paid for a replica [Figure 55]. In the same year, Jefferson engaged Brown to paint Adams (Boston Athenaeum) and, a year later, Thomas Paine, author of *Common Sense* (appar-

Figure 54.
William Woollett
Gilbert Stuart
Oil on canvas, 1783
90.2 x 69.8 cm. (35½ x 27½ in.)
The Trustees of The Tate Gallery, London

Figure 55.
Thomas Jefferson
Mather Brown
Oil on canvas, 1786
90.8 x 71.1 cm. (35¾ x 28 in.)
Charles Francis Adams
Not in exhibition

ently never executed). Mather Brown exhibited more frequently at the Royal Academy than his early mentor, and, after Stuart's departure for Ireland in 1787, began to receive increased public recognition. He produced highly successful fulllengths of the monarch's sons, the *Prince of Wales* (Her Majesty Queen Elizabeth II) and the *Duke of York* [Figure 56], in 1788, and, on this basis, was appointed official portrait painter to the Duke of York.

Naturally the success of the Americans was galling to their British counterparts. One of them wrote, during the summer of 1789: *Mr. West paints for the Court and Mr. Copley for the City. Thus the artists of America are fostered in England, and to complete the wonder, a third American, Mr. Brown of the humblest pretences, is chosen portrait painter to the Duke of York. So much for*

Figure 56.
Duke of York
Mather Brown
Oil on canvas, 1788
216.8 x 129.6 cm. (85¼ x 51 in.)
The National Trust for Places of
Historic Interest or Natural Beauty,
Waddesdon Manor, England
Not in exhibition

the Thirteen Stripes—so much for the Duke of York's taste.[17]

With renewed determination, John Trumbull returned to England after peace was declared and, by the spring of 1784, was "the established successor of Gilbert Stuart in West's apartments."[18] Setting up his easel in the Newman Street studio, he worked there daily. He used this address when he exhibited at the Royal Academy, but he was not actually in residence. During the evenings he went to the Academy to sketch. *The Dancing Faun* [Figure 57], inscribed with a date of

Figure 57.
The Dancing Faun
John Trumbull
Black and white chalk, October 1784
49.7 x 31.5 cm. (19 9/16 x 12 3/8 in.)
Cooper-Hewitt Museum,
Smithsonian Institution

Figure 58.
*Jeremiah Wadsworth and
His Son, Daniel*
John Trumbull
Oil on canvas, 1784
90.2 x 69.2 cm. (35½ x 27¼ in.)
Wadsworth Atheneum, Hartford
Not in exhibition

October 1784 and revealing a beginner's struggle over proportions, is one of his surviving black-and-white chalk drawings from the Academy's casts. Some of his studies from live models also exist (Fordham University) and were probably done after he was officially enrolled as a student on March 22, 1785.

Trumbull summoned up his courage at about this time and brought a small whole-length of his friends, *Jeremiah Wadsworth and His Son, Daniel* [Figure 58], to the Academy's president for an opinion. Reynolds's immediate reaction, with a severity that Trumbull was not used to, was, "That coat is bad, sir, very bad; it is not cloth—it is tin, bent tin." Not the sort of man to take such criticisms easily, Trumbull replied, with an air of feigned superiority, "I did not bring this

84

thing to you, Sir Joshua, merely to be told that it is bad; I was conscious of that ... I had a hope that you would kindly have pointed out to me, how to correct my errors."[19] He never went to Reynolds again.

Writing to his brother on March 10, 1784, Trumbull described a contrasting reaction when he submitted "a portrait of Mr. Temple as a specimen for Mr. West's judgment & advice. He was pleas'd to commend it in warm terms and to give me much encouragement to persevere in the Art."[20] The three-quarter-length of *Sir John Temple* [Figure 59], in its greater softness and fluidity, shows a marked advancement over the Wadsworth portrait; but, as Stuart pointed out,

Figure 59.
Sir John Temple
John Trumbull
Oil on canvas, 1784
90.1 x 97.8 cm. (50½ x 38½ in.)
Canajoharie Library and Art Gallery, New York

Figure 60.
Battle of La Hogue
Benjamin West and John Trumbull
Oil on canvas, 1784–85
163.8 x 243.8 cm. (64½ x 96 in.)
The Metropolitan Museum of Art,
New York, Harris Brisbane Dick
Fund, 1964
Not in exhibition

"West gave positive and Reynolds negative instruction."[21] Trumbull was so pleased that he exhibited his picture at the Royal Academy that year.

His closing remark, in this same letter to his brother, is especially significant: "The late [American] war opens a new & noble field for historical painting."[22] This was precisely West's opinion. Almost a year earlier, in June of 1783, he had written to Charles Willson Peale, congratulating him on a victory that would enshrine the names of his countrymen "for ever among the greatest characters of antiquity," and asking him to send drawings of the uniforms of the Continental Army "to enable me to form a few pictures of the great events of the American contest . . . which I propose to have engraved." He would call the series "The American Revolution."[23] Undoubtedly in deference to the king, West eventually dropped the idea and encouraged Trumbull to take it up.

After working as an assistant, copying West's *Death of Wolfe* (copy unlocated) and the 1778 *Battle of La Hogue* [copy, Figure 60], which was of "inestimable importance" to his development,[24] Trumbull tried an original, historical composition of *Priam Returning with the Body of Hector* [Figure 61]. He definitely felt more secure with a relatively small canvas (24¾ x 36¾ inches), rather than the size to which West was accustomed. As the result of a childhood accident, Trumbull had sight only in his right eye; and his background had been largely in painting miniatures. West, moreover, advised him to keep to a reduced scale.[25] Although the young artist evidently paid for models for his picture,[26] the pose of the dead Hector is clearly derived from that of Stephen in West's altarpiece for St. Stephen's, Walbrook; the vignette of the mother with two children to the left is a West favorite (his *Departure of Regulus* [Figure 24]); and the facial types, particularly the classically stereotyped women, are all related to West's generic heads. The use of these types, with rhetorical gestures, was a common means of clarifying the narrative by making the characters of the figures more easily readable. Trumbull's creamy thick highlights, loosely suggested edges, and Rubensesque color, seen in *Priam* and considered typical of his best style, are partially enriched by glazing which could also be an influence from West. According to Trumbull's notes from a conversation in 1784, West taught him to glaze with complementary colors to produce "an astonishing degree of Union & Brilliance." This rule, West observed, was "founded in Nature." If, for example, *a Blue drapery is found to be too powerfull & glittering for the other parts, & you wish it to be lower'd, this cannot be done by glazing with Blue, for that will but encrease the glitter. It cannot be glaz'd with Black without producing a Mudiness—Red will produce a purple & Yellow gives a Green:—but Orange in which are contain'd the two remaining Primitives, will at once reduce the*

Figure 61.
Priam Returning with the Body of Hector
John Trumbull
Oil on canvas, 1785
62.9 x 93.3 cm. (24¾ x 36¾ in.)
The Virginia Museum of Fine Arts, Richmond

Figure 62.
The Death of General Warren at the Battle of Bunker's Hill, June 17, 1775
John Trumbull
Oil on canvas, 1786
63.5 x 86.3 cm. (25 x 34 in.)
Yale University Art Gallery,
New Haven,
Mabel Brady Garvan Collection
Not in exhibition

Colour to the depth requir'd.[27] Trumbull's consciousness of color balance in his distribution of primaries also reflects the contemporary practice of his master, as in his huge and dramatically impressive *Last Supper* [Figure 4], commissioned by George III in 1786 as an altarpiece for St. George's Chapel in Windsor.

West's coloring, however, was never his best point, as he himself realized. It could be strong and decorative, but it lacked the subtle richness and transparency already evident in Trumbull's *Priam*. On the few occasions when his opinion on color was recorded, he gave very basic instructions, helpful for any student, such as in the use of warm and cool colors respectively in light and dark areas of a painting. He recommended that the dominant colors be treated as "focii" against a background containing gentler echos of those pigments. One of the themes that he stressed was that the artist should be conscious of the corresponding values of different hues so that he would always be aware of whether a color receded or projected. Basically, he emphasized the importance of an effect of harmony, and continued, like most of his English contemporaries, to experiment with glazes in the hope of being able to duplicate the effects of the Venetians.[28]

When *Priam* was exhibited at the Royal Academy in 1786, one critic commented that it was "a considerable advance" over Trumbull's previous contributions: "The colouring is more brilliant, and we think we foresee much improvement of this young artist in *character*, which will greatly assist his pencil."[29]

Recognition such as this prompted Trumbull to begin to think more seriously about a series on the American Revolution. Having participated as a soldier, he was exceptionally well qualified for such an undertaking. With West's support, and in West's studio, he started in 1785 with *The Death of General Warren at the Battle of Bunker's Hill* [Figure 62], followed by *The Death of General Montgomery in the Attack on Quebec* [Figure 63], two very fine, small diagonal compositions which, in the whirling blend of forms and battle colors, make their precedent, West's *Death of General Wolfe* [Figure 1], look static and too self-consciously staged. "To speak of its merit," Abigail Adams remarked, in her judgment of *Bunker's Hill*, "I can only say that in looking at it my whole frame contracted, my blood shivered, and I felt a faintness at my heart."[30] Before Trumbull had finished the second episode, Copley joined West in urging him to have the series engraved. The esteem in which Copley was held as a history painter lent weight to his argument. His *Death of Major Peirson* [Figure 64],

Figure 63.
The Death of General Montgomery in the Attack on Quebec, December 31, 1775
John Trumbull
Oil on canvas, 1786
63.5 x 86.3 cm. (25 x 34 in.)
Yale University Art Gallery,
New Haven,
Mabel Brady Garvan Collection
Not in exhibition

Figure 64.
The Death of Major Peirson
John Singleton Copley
Oil on canvas, 1782–84
264.4 x 365.8 cm. (97 x 144 in.)
The Trustees of The Tate Gallery, London
Not in exhibition

showing a heroic British officer dying at the hands of the French, was, like his earlier *Death of the Earl of Chatham* [Figure 65], exhibited outside the Royal Academy in 1784 as a one-man show with an admission charge. The tactic was highly successful. Subscriptions for engravings after Copley's pictures were still being taken as a further commercial venture. West, Trumbull said, explained to him, "with the kindness of a father, all the intricacies of such an enterprise—the choice of engravers, printers, publisher, &c. &c."[31]

Trumbull's first two scenes were not without controversy. Although Bunker Hill was an American victory, the picture compromises by depicting the British, in a winning position, displaying humanity towards a fallen American. Likewise, *The Death of Montgomery* has mixed loyalties in that the American is represented dying heroically in the midst of what was a defeat. This ambivalence was intended for wider appeal, but it caused the American Congress, years later, to refuse to commission enlargements.

The cost of having these two pictures engraved, about a thousand pounds, was discouraging, but the profit from the sale of the prints could, on the other hand, be expected to pay for engraving the rest of the series. Fortunately, a wealthy friend lent his money to subsidize the project; West found Antonio di

Poggi who would advance all the money for a share in the print sales; and Trumbull, meanwhile, had the advantage of being well paid for his assistance on West's commissions from the king. In December of 1786, West even offered him a thousand or fifteen-hundred pounds for help on "some other things," but Trumbull hesitated, "lest it should interrupt me too much."[32]

    His period of apprenticeship under West was about as long as Stuart's. Although Trumbull had greater financial and social backing than Stuart, his chosen career as a history painter was much more precarious. He must have lingered with trepidation. As Dunlap realized, even though Trumbull made the illustration of the Revolution his life's work, his best historical pictures were actually completed under West. He worked on sketches for several in the series, and then, at West's suggestion in 1786,[33] decided to try to carry British favor by depicting the English repulse of the Spanish attack in 1782 at Gibraltar. His first idea, *The Siege of Gibraltar*, was evidently discarded after the initial sketch because it was a subject upon which Copley was also working. His second choice was an incident that took place almost a year earlier than the siege, in 1781, when the British

Figure 65.
The Death of the Earl of Chatham
John Singleton Copley
Oil on canvas, 1779–81
228.4 x 307.2 cm. (90 x 121 in.)
The Trustees of The Tate Gallery, London
Not in exhibition

Figure 66.
The Sortie Made by the Garrison of Gibraltar, November 27, 1781
John Trumbull
Oil on canvas, 1789
178 x 264.2 cm. (67¼ x 104 in.)
The Metropolitan Museum of Art, New York, Pauline V. Fullerton Bequest; Mr. and Mrs. James Walter Carter Gift; Mr. and Mrs. Raymond J. Horowitz Gift; Erving Wolf Foundation Gift; Vain and Harry Fish Foundation, Inc., Gift; Gift of Hanson K. Corning, by exchange; and Maria DeWitt Jesup and Morris K. Jesup Funds, 1976
Not in exhibition

sent out a night sortie to destroy the breastworks of the Spanish offensive.

The first small oil sketch for *The Sortie Made by the Garrison of Gibraltar* (Corcoran Gallery of Art) was presented to West in gratitude for his aid. The second version, incorporating some changes and containing more portraits, was really a finished work (1788; Cincinnati Art Museum) and the basis for the huge, final masterpiece (1789 [Figure 66; color, page 127]). Trumbull's awareness of the dramatic potential of spotlighting was already evident in his earlier history painting, and here, again, he uses his highlights with unusual skill. The brilliant conflagration behind, the silhouetted axe, and the bloodstained knife all add to a sensational impact. Despite his difficulty in working on such a scale, Trumbull's large *Sortie* was hailed as a triumph. In its fluid brushwork and fresh coloring, it comes somewhat closer to Copley's English style than to West's; and its composition is more effectively cohesive than West's contemporary 1788 *Battle of Crécy* (Her Majesty Queen Elizabeth II). The different versions show that he changed the body of the dying Spaniard in the center so that it more closely approximated the Royal Academy cast of the *Dying Gladiator* and thus finally read as a fashionable quotation from classical art.

Following Copley's precedent, Trumbull rented a hall in Spring Gardens for a one-man display of his gigantic picture. Aside from the admission charge, this would bring in subscriptions for an engraving. Trumbull's grand historical picture, with an elaborate frame, backed by a scarlet curtain, had to compete with the dual attractions of the Royal Academy's spring exhibition and Boydell's Shakespeare Gallery. Since he did not have a picture in either of these shows, the challenge was that much greater. The novelty of the Shakespeare Gallery, containing large oils commissioned from leading artists to illustrate England's renowned dramatist, was expected to draw crowds. All works were to be engraved for John Boydell's edition of Shakespeare. But, even after Trumbull's painting had been on view for almost two months, a June newspaper reported that it "is still resorted to by the Military and the Fair; indeed a picture of so much beauty and excellence has not been offered since *Copley's* Lord *Chatham*."[34] On the strength of such praise, Trumbull returned to the United States in December of 1789 to collect portraits of surviving officers for his series and subscriptions for the engravings.

According to the terminology of the day, there were lower forms of the history picture, which included literary illustrations, such as those in the Shakespeare Gallery, and some portraits and landscapes. The "historical portrait" usually entailed a full-length size, trappings signifying rank, and a noble posture which gave it pretensions to grandeur that an ordinary likeness did not have. On the other hand, West's *Telemachus and Calypso* [Figure 111] was a "historical landscape" in the sense that its primary focus was on a landscape with a secondary use of a classical subject. These hybrid pictures, encouraged by Reynolds in his Fourth Discourse (1771), in which he urged portrait and landscape painters to upgrade their subjects by borrowing elements from the Grand Style of historical painting, were symptomatic of a general confusion surrounding the term "history painting," mostly because the expression was associated with vague ideas of high quality. Definitions of "history painting" were never really fixed, and attempts to define the term only led to a self-defeating tendency to separate the category into subdivisions or branches, but the public never understood these refinements, and the label was, in fact, loosely used even by artists to cover all narrative pictures with serious content.

While Trumbull labored over his history pictures on speculation, Brown earned his living outside West's studio as a portraitist, and longed to be admired as a history painter. Unlike most of the other protégés, Brown spent his life in England and, even after he left the Newman Street studio, he was never really free of West's influence. His first chance came in 1784. He received a rare public commission then for two canvases, each a little less than eight feet high, of the *Passion of Our Saviour in the Garden of Gethsemane* [Figure 67] and the *Annunciation of the Virgin* for the chancel of the New Church (St. Mary's) in the Strand. Despite his youth (twenty-three), Brown rose to the occasion with two superbly imaginative works inspired by West's latest pictures (1784) in the Revealed Religion series for the King's private chapel at Windsor. The flame-like hair on the angel in the *Passion of Our Savior* appears so distinctive, and yet

Figure 67.
Passion of Our Saviour in the Garden of Gethsemane
Mather Brown
Oil on canvas, 1784
223.6 x 97.8 cm. (88 x 38½ in.)
St. Mary-le-Strand Church, London
Not in exhibition

Figure 68.
The Call of Isaiah
Benjamin West
Oil on canvas, 1784
381 x 154.9 cm. (150 x 61 in.)
Bob Jones University Collection,
Greenville, South Carolina
Not in exhibition

it is seen in West's *Call of Isaiah* [Figure 68]; the raised arm of the angel in Brown's *Annunciation* is also from the same messenger in West's *Isaiah*; and the putti recall those in West's intended companion piece of *The Call of Jeremiah* (sketch, Musée des Beaux-Arts, Bordeaux). Coming from a background of distinguished Boston theologians and having posed for one of West's Revealed Religion scenes (an *Ascension*, in 1782), Brown was especially impressed with that series. On his own, and given free rein, he produced a gentler variation.

Figure 69.
Lord Howe on the Deck of the "Queen Charlotte"
Daniel Orme, after Mather Brown
Engraving, 1795
48.3 x 60.7 cm. (19 x 23⅞ in.)
National Maritime Museum, London

Like Trumbull with his *George Washington*, Mather Brown apparently contacted Valentine Green to engrave his St. Mary-le-Strand pictures in mezzotint; and, like Trumbull with Poggi, Brown eventually formed a business partnership with another artist, Daniel Orme, for the exhibition, sale, and engraving of Brown's historical pictures. From 1792 to about 1797, Orme exhibited these scenes in his print shop and engraved most of them. Since they were designed as a speculative enterprise—to be advertised in the newspapers, to attract crowds, and to elicit subscriptions for an engraving—such pictures were shown in one-man displays rather than with possible competition at the Royal Academy. Brown continued to lend his portraits to the Academy, but his history pictures were all reserved for Orme's gallery.

To ensure success with a proposition dependent upon the sale of engravings, it was imperative to capture the public's imagination. Perhaps, then, it was inevitable that, during a time of war, history painters would turn to current events with dramatic potential. At first, past actions were portrayed, and then, increasingly in the 1790s, artists competed with each other to produce a commemorative picture as soon as possible after the event.

The popularity of prints after his work drove Brown to seek new topics in current events during the 1790s. His dramatic "reportage" pictures are of the same type as Trumbull's Revolutionary War scenes, but the figures are usually larger in proportion to the background, and there is very often a stage effect, as if Brown could never quite shake the influence of the Shakespeare Gallery. One of his last such pictures was his celebration of the maritime victory of Admiral Howe over the French fleet on the "Glorious First" of June 1794, an incident which catapulted Howe onto the plateau of a great national hero. Engravings after the subject were expected to ride the wave of patriotism occasioned by the Napoleonic Wars. Rather than paint a distant seascape, Brown strove to move the emotions, in the manner of West's heroic painting, with a universal theme— the personal tragedy of war. He focused on the death of the young Captain Neville of the Queen's Royal Regiment in his *Lord Howe on the Deck of the "Queen Charlotte"* [Figure 69]. When the picture was exhibited at Orme's gallery, a contemporary reported that it was considered "a good naval subject, and well adapted to the feelings of the public on the occasion. Everyone went to see it."[35]

Almost, but not all, of Brown's historical pictures were painted on speculation. The Duke of Norfolk, for instance, commissioned a group of canvases for Arundel Castle depicting the exploits of his famous ancestors. One of them was *The Duke of Norfolk Receiving from Henry VIII an Augmentation to His Coat-of-Arms in Consequence of the Victory of Flodden Field, 1513*, shown at the Royal Academy in 1797 (unlocated), and another was the theatrical *Thomas, Earl of Surrey, Son of John, 1st Duke of Norfolk, Defending His Allegiance to Richard*

Figure 70.
Thomas, Earl of Surrey, Son of John, 1st Duke of Norfolk, Defending His Allegiance to Richard III before Henry VII after the Battle of Bosworth Field, 1485
Mather Brown
Oil on canvas, circa 1797
199.7 x 294.1 cm. (78⅝ x 115¾ in.)
His Grace the Duke of Norfolk, CB.

Figure 71.
Cromwell Dissolving the Long Parliament
Benjamin West
Oil on canvas, 1782
152.4 x 213.4 cm. (60 x 84 in.)
Montclair Art Museum, New Jersey,
Members Acquisition Fund, 1960

III before Henry VII after the Battle of Bosworth Field, 1485 [Figure 70; color, page 128]. A splendid costume piece, with flamboyant gestures and the bright color of pageantry, the surviving painting is strongly reminiscent of Benjamin's West's 1782 *Cromwell Dissolving the Long Parliament* [Figure 71], part of a series on English history painted for the Earl of Grosvenor.

Late in life, Brown gravitated closer to West's sphere of influence, with large religious pictures which, like the early ones for St. Mary-le-Strand, bear the indelible imprint of "the American Raphael." Saddened and impoverished by the financial depression that accompanied and succeeded the Napoleonic Wars, he took up his brush to follow the successes of West's late *Christ Healing the Sick in the Temple* [Figure 5] and *Christ Rejected by the Jews* [Figure 6] with a number of missing religious compositions. The only known, surviving representative of the group is the 1824 *Finding of Moses* [Figure 72]. Like Trumbull, Brown often employed facial types in his imaginary subjects that derived from West. The women, for example, in the *Finding of Moses* are taken from the anonymous, classical ideal so often used by West, and the artificial surface sheen on their garments is characteristic of the older artist. Brown so admired his master's scriptural subjects that he is reputed to have remarked that "he worshiped them by day, and they were even before him as delightful visions of the night."[36] He was barely able to eke out a living as a failing artist in Manchester when he learned of West's death in 1820, but, with the devotion of a true disciple, he responded with a burst of history painting. His 1825 oil sketch for *The Battle of the Nile* [Figure 73], commemorating Nelson's decisive victory over the French off the coast of Egypt, showed that he still had a powerful creative imagination at age sixty-four. He wrote home to Boston in poverty and pitiful delusion: "When West dropped the Mantle I caught it up."[37]

Figure 72.
Finding of Moses
Mather Brown
Oil on canvas, 1824
121.9 x 99.1 cm. (48 x 39 in.)
Mrs. Johan Koppernaes
Not in exhibition

Figure 73.
Oil Sketch for The Battle of the Nile
Mather Brown
Oil on canvas, 1825
100.3 x 123.2 cm. (39½ x 48½ in.)
National Maritime Museum, London

Perhaps the most curious phenomenon in the development of West's students is the fact that both Brown and Trumbull, the two artists who were the most closely linked stylistically to West, went through a second phase of West's influence in the early nineteenth century, which was stronger than while they were his pupils in the 1780s. When Trumbull returned to painting in England in 1800, after a short diplomatic career of about seven years, he based his portrait style on West's. With a new fondness for black shadows, rather opaque colors, and shiny metallic textures, he adopted the worst characteristics of West's later work. He also followed the older artist's lead in subject matter and began to concentrate on Biblical scenes, as in his *Infant Saviour with St. John the Baptist Dressing the Lamb with Flowers* (1801 [Figure 74]) or in his *Our Saviour with Little Children* (1812, Yale University Art Gallery), where the character types and emotional gestures stem from West.

Figure 74.
*Infant Saviour with
St. John the Baptist
Dressing the Lamb with Flowers*
John Trumbull
Oil on canvas, 1801
76.1 x 64.7 cm. (30⅛ x 25³⁄₁₆ in.)
Wadsworth Atheneum, Hartford,
Gift of Samuel C. Perkins

With regard to drawing style, Benjamin West was notoriously changeable, and there is really only one student, other than his sons, whose identifying characteristics remained consistently close to him. That is to say that Brown's lifelong manner in figure sketching might well have derived from West's idiom of the 1780s. One of the most interesting comparisons appears when these two artists treat the same subject. Mather Brown's *Moses Striking the Rock* [Figure 75], from probably the 1790s, in character typing and theatrical gesture resembles West's drawing of the same title (1788 [Figure 76]); but the similarity goes much deeper. Both artists enjoy the delineation of muscular form and almost any excuse for a broken, curvilinear line which becomes at times just a squiggle. They also occasionally exaggerate an expressive hand so that it is oversized. This is a characteristic also found at times in Trumbull's work, as in his *Deluge* [Figure 77].

Figure 75.
Moses Striking the Rock
Mather Brown
Ink and wash, 1790s
41.2 x 56.5 cm. (16¼ x 22¼ in.)
The estate of Walter Brandt

Figure 76.
Moses Striking the Rock
Benjamin West
Ink and gouache, 1788;
retouched 1803
58.4 x 111.8 cm. (23 x 44 in.)
Royal Academy of Arts,
London

Figure 77.
The Deluge
John Trumbull
Ink and wash, 1786
11.7 x 13.9 cm. (4⅝ x 5½ in.)
Fordham University Library,
New York

The known, documented works by West's son, Raphael Lamar West (1766-1850), consist of only a few drawings and prints, but these are enough to place him—with Brown, Trumbull, and possibly Robert Fulton—in the class of those most visibly affected by Benjamin West. Raphael's reputation for idleness suggests that the lost oils, even if found, would be very limited in number. He worked on some of his father's larger canvases, but he and his younger brother, Benjamin, Jr. [Figure 78], apparently never really contributed to lessening the household expenses (no work has been conclusively assigned to Benjamin, Jr.).[38] The elder brother's pen-and-ink sketches of the action-packed *Cadmus Slaying the Dragon*

Raphael Lamar West

Figure 78.
Raphael and Benjamin West, Sons of the Artist
Benjamin West
Oil on canvas, probably 1796
89.5 x 71.7 cm. (35¼ x 28¼ in.)
Nelson Gallery-Atkins Museum,
Kansas City, Missouri,
Gift of the Laura Nelson Kirkwood Residuary Trust

Figure 79.
Cadmus Slaying the Dragon
Raphael Lamar West
Ink and graphite on paper,
possibly 1785
29.7 x 22.5 cm. (11¹¹⁄₁₆ x 8⅞ in.)
The Pierpont Morgan Library,
New York

Figure 80.
Brigand Lying Under a Tree
Raphael Lamar West
Ink over black chalk on paper, possibly 1785
38.1 x 25.9 cm. (15 x 10³⁄₁₆ in.)
The Pierpont Morgan Library,
New York

[Figure 79] and the brooding *Brigand Lying Under a Tree* [Figure 80] can be stylistically related to the father; yet Raphael's line is almost uncontrollably loose, and there is a general sloppiness in anatomical detail, particularly in representing hands and feet. His drawing has some of his father's dramatic power but without the kind of controlled strength and confident ability that is so evident in Benjamin West's splendid *Angel in the Sun* [Figure 81]. Raphael's best picture was reputed to be his *Orlando Rescuing Oliver from the Lion and the Serpent*, a commission for Boydell's Shakespeare Gallery taken from Act IV of *As You Like it*. Preserved in the form of an engraving [Figure 82] by William Charles Wilson, published in 1798, the composition shows Orlando—under an enormous and rather fantastically gnarled oak—advancing in a pose roughly dependent upon Benjamin West's 1793 *Diomed and His Horses Stopped by the Lightning of Jupiter* (formerly J. Leger and Sons). But, with a dark and menacing setting, Raphael has given the subject, as a friend pointed out, his own distinct mark "in the taste of Salvator Rosa."[39]

Figure 81.
Angel in the Sun
Benjamin West
Ink and gouache, circa 1795/98
34.3 x 27.9 cm. (13½ x 11 in.)
The Toledo Museum of Art,
Gift of Edward Drummond Libbey

Figure 82.
Orlando Rescuing Oliver from the Lion and the Serpent
William Charles Wilson,
after Raphael Lamar West
Engraving, 1798
43.8 x 58.7 cm. (17¼ x 23⅛ in.)
The Folger Shakespeare Library,
Washington, D.C.

Thomas Spence Duché

Not much is known about the other American artists who were with West during the 1780s. One of them, the young Philadelphian Thomas Spence Duché (1763-1790) showed promise but was suffering from tuberculosis which finally caused his death.[40] His mother took him to London in 1780 to join his Loyalist father, the Reverend Jacob Duché; and, by April of 1783, the elder Duché was able to report that his son was *a Pupil of my good Friend West.... And his great Example has excited in my Boy an Ambition to distinguish himself in his Native Country.... The late Revolution has opened a large Field for Design. His young mind already teems with the great Subjects of Councils, Senates, Heroes, Battles.* Two months later, he added that "Money seems not to be his Object but Fame—He has the Presumption to aspire after Excellence, in the Historical Line—and to think too meanly of Portraits."[41] Duché's earliest datable portrait, completed in this year, is of his sister, *Esther Duché* [Figure 83]. The face, with the idealized, introverted appearance of a classical cast, is carefully outlined and then brushed in with delicate color so that it retains the aspect of a drawing. On the other hand, the dress is so freely rendered, in the fashionable, loose manner, that it appears to have a turbulent life of its own. The same outlining and somewhat awkward anatomy are seen in his other works. Duché planned to ship the likeness of his sister to his aunt, since "it is generally thought very like," but he hesitated because "I would not send it," he wrote, "without M‍r West's approbation, & he is very particular in those of my pictures that are going to P-a."[42] Duché's likenesses, chiefly of visiting Philadelphians or family members, like the tondo portrait of himself with his father [Figure 84], are often on a relatively small canvas. His other documented subjects are allegorical scenes, on this same reduced scale, and include a pair engraved after his death, of *Hope Delivering Two Orphan Girls to the Genius of the Asylum* (Sabin Galleries, Ltd., London) and *Charity Presenting a Prostitute to Three Reclaimed Females at the Magdalen Hospital* (unlocated).[43] Perhaps under West's inspiration, he traveled to Paris with a fellow-Philadelphian in May of 1788. According to an introductory letter

Figure 83.
Esther Duché
Thomas Spence Duché
Oil on canvas, 1783
56.8 x 45.7 cm. (22⅜ x 18 in.)
The Historical Society of
Pennsylvania, Philadelphia

from Trumbull to Jefferson, he intended at that time to take up historical painting and to portray events in American history, apparently in emulation of Trumbull.[44] His illness sapped his strength to such an extent, however, that he finally had to give up his artistic career in 1789.

Figure 84.
Thomas Spence Duché and His Father Jacob
Thomas Spence Duché
Oil on canvas, circa 1784/85
45.7 x 45.7 cm. (18 x 18 in.)
The Historical Society of Pennsylvania, Philadelphia

West's importance is underlined by the fact that Duché paid to have one of his portraits, the *Reverend Samuel Seabury* [Figure 85], engraved by William Sharp and published in 1786 with a dedication to his master "affectionately inscribed by His grateful Friend & Pupil." Certainly he must have thought that the Seabury likeness documented an improvement for which he felt indebted. Compared to the portrait of *Esther*, it has a much broader treatment and, instead of the blanket shadow on one side of the head, there is more skillful modeling

Figure 85.
Reverend Samuel Seabury
Thomas Spence Duché
Oil on canvas, 1785
127 x 101.6 cm. (50 x 40 in.)
Trinity College, Hartford

Figure 86.
Portrait of an Unknown Gentleman
James Earl
Oil on canvas, circa 1784/94
76.2 x 63.5 cm. (30 x 25 in.)
Bowdoin College Museum of Art,
Brunswick, Maine
Not in exhibition

and a sensitive observation of secondary highlights. The pose, forceful and commanding, is here cleverly used to convey the character of the first Episcopal bishop of Connecticut. Under West's gentle prodding, Duché's portraits were brought more into line with the high British standard, but his hopes in the historical area were never to be realized.

It has been assumed that James Earl (1761-1796), the younger brother of Ralph, studied under Benjamin West,[45] but there is no evidence for this one way or the other. In fact, there is some reason to doubt it. Although his life is shrouded in mystery, a 1796 obituary notice says that he was in London for ten years before his departure in 1794 for Charleston, South Carolina;[46] yet William Dunlap, our invaluable historian, was in West's circle from June of 1784 to August of

1787 and never met Earl. He neither included him in his list of West's pupils nor even recognized his name when he repeated a brief account of him, second-hand, in his *History of the Rise and Progress of the Arts of Design in the United States*.[47] Possibly Earl worked outside London, as his brother had done, before he exhibited *A Small Head* and *Two Boys* (both unlocated) at the Royal Academy in 1787. Unlike his brother, however, he followed a more ambitious path through the Academy schools, which he entered on March 24, 1789. His English work, represented by a *Portrait of an Unknown Gentleman* [Figure 86] and *Lady Caroline Beauclerk*,[48] shown at the Royal Academy in 1790, are indicative of an unusually fine talent which came to full fruition in Britain. But there is nothing in his *oeuvre* which convincingly ties him to West.

When the rather jaunty and dapper William Dunlap (1766-1839) crossed the Atlantic in 1784 from New Jersey, he brought specimens of his work to show West. His portfolio is typical of what West was used to receiving: a drawing from the print of Copley's *Watson and the Shark* (Dunlap was somewhat embarrassed that it was not his copy after the print of West's *Death of General Wolfe*) and a larger picture, his second attempt in oils, of *Washington at Princeton* (both unlocated), which would certainly please because the dying General Mercer in the background imitated West's depiction of Wolfe. The master was not as impressed as Dunlap had hoped. But, of the last, he observed, "This shows some talent for composition,"[49] and he offered to lend Dunlap his casts for drawing practice.

William Dunlap

Dunlap, however, was easily swayed from his purpose. Supported by his parents, he readily accepted dinner invitations from West, but the delights of London were too seductive for him to concentrate on drawing from casts. "A long residence in London," Dunlap later admitted with the sobering of age, "left me ignorant of anatomy, perspective, drawing, and colouring, and returned me home a most incapable painter."[50] Instead, "the theatres—Vauxhall—parties on foot to Richmond-hill and on horseback to Windsor, and every dissipation suggested by my companions or myself, was eagerly entered into."[51] Raphael West, Dunlap found, was always ready to be amused and was one of the first to join the more idle group.

Dunlap made a few attempts at history painting, which included a copy of West's 1764 *Choice of Hercules* and an original composition of *Ferrau Gazing with Horror upon the Ghost* (both unlocated) from Ariosto's *Orlando Furioso*; but most of his limited work, at this time, consisted of portraits of his friends. He described the best one (unidentified) as "freely touched, well coloured, and full of expression," but he had to agree with West's objection that the two sides of the figure were too much alike, "like a rolling pin."[52] Although all of his English pictures are missing, *The Artist Showing a Picture from "Hamlet" to His Parents* [Figure 87], painted about 1788 after his return to America, shows that his style, compared to his 1783 pastel bust of Washington [Figure 88], had changed little as the result of his sojourn abroad. He was able to create an effective group composition, but this may reflect only his prior talent, upon which West had remarked. The picture is an advertisement of his artistic accomplish-

Figure 87.
The Artist Showing a Picture from "Hamlet" to His Parents
William Dunlap
Oil on canvas, circa 1788
107.3 x 124.4 cm. (42¼ x 49 in.)
The New-York Historical Society,
Gift of John Crumby

George William West

ments. Within the format of a conversation piece, Dunlap has demonstrated that he could paint not only an acceptable portrait but a history picture as sublime as the one shown to his approving father and apprehensive mother. The figures are characteristically "freely touched" with a somewhat uncertain, feathery, dry stroke, producing an effect similar to the pastel chalks that had been his medium before London. They also lack the definition and substance that West would have preferred.

The English work of two other students in the Newman Street studio is unfortunately lost: George William West (1770-1795), who came from Baltimore in 1788, and Henry Sargent, who arrived from Boston in 1793. Young "Billy" West (no relation), according to a manuscript history of St. Paul's Parish, Baltimore, written about 1850, had intended to stay in London for three years before going on to Italy, but, before the end of eighteen months, he became ill and had to return home in the fall of 1790.[53] He died of tuberculosis five years later. All that definitely survives from his London period is a sheet of paper containing three rough pencil sketches of figures observed from life [Figure 89], drawn very much in the manner of a beginner.

According to Dunlap, Henry Sargent (1770-1845) was a late bloomer, or rather, the "faculty for imitating forms remained dormant, and the craniological bump undeveloped."[54] His early instructor in art, the man who successfully diverted him from his mercantile career, was John Johnston.[55] It was to Johnston, a portraitist who worked out of an artisan tradition, that Sargent wished to be remembered when he wrote home from London.[56] But he would never have embarked for England in 1793 if it had not been for "the Strong recommendations" of John Trumbull, then in Boston, who gave him introductory letters to West and Samuel Jennings, a little-known Philadelphia artist in London.[57]

Like Dunlap, Sargent does not seem to have benefited artistically from the English experience. Those of his letters that survive from this period do not mention West. Instead he writes, in March of 1795, to William Lovett, an amateur miniaturist in Boston, that "Painting is very dull here." In answer to Lovett's request for information on how to paint a miniature, he relays the advice of "my friend Mr [John Edmund] Halpin [a somewhat obscure miniature painter] who is one of the greatest painters if not the greatest."[58] He did manage to exhibit twice at the Royal Academy, a portrait of a *Mr. Hanger* in 1795 and

Henry Sargent

Figure 88.
George Washington
William Dunlap
Pastel, 1783
64.8 x 49.5 cm. (25½ x 19½ in.), sight
United States Capitol, Gift of
Mrs. A. V. H. Ellis, 1940
Not in exhibition

Figure 89.
Figure Sketches
George William West
Graphite on paper, 1788/90
14.6 x 19.4 cm. (5¾ x 7⅝ in.)
Museum and Library of Maryland History/Maryland Historical Society, Baltimore

a literary piece, from a ballad by Oliver Goldsmith, of *Edwin and Angelina* (both unlocated) in 1796. The last, he acknowledged, "looks in the exhibition like *a taper light amidst a World* of Suns—But it serves to admit me to see the exhibition *gratis* as often as I choose to go."[59] His later letters convey a growing dissatisfaction, for he had constantly to economize because of his financial dependence upon his parents, and he did not feel that he was gaining from the venture. Whereas—and here he was reflecting the views of his well-traveled friend, Trumbull—"there is no better school in the *World*—than at present there is in *Paris*." He explained that the private collections of Old Masters in Paris were more accessible and an artist could copy there "*free of expense*." He urged his parents to send him there so that he could "see more of the world."[60] The Sargents, however, were not convinced; he returned to Boston in 1797.

Figure 91.
Judge David Sewall
John Johnston
Oil on canvas, 1790
89.8 x 70.8 cm. (35⅜ x 27⅞ in.)
Bowdoin College Museum of Art,
Brunswick, Maine
Not in exhibition

Figure 90.
Captain Joseph McLellan, Sr.
Henry Sargent
Oil on canvas, 1798
75.5 x 62.9 cm. (29¾ x 24¾ in.)
Portland Museum of Art, Maine

Although none of Sargent's English work is known to survive, the portraits that he executed just after his return are so close to John Johnston's work that it is obvious that he did not take full advantage of his opportunity. West opened his studio, but, as Dunlap discovered, he did not feel "authorized to control and advise" those who came to him unless they sought help.[61] Sargent's *Captain Joseph McLellan, Sr.* [Figure 90], signed and dated 1798, is surprisingly reminiscent of John Johnston's *Judge David Sewall* [Figure 91]. The same breadth in lights and shadows seen in *McLellan*, which produces a flatness, is what Sargent had appreciated in Halpin's work,[62] and the rather crude drawing is more related to sign and ornamental painting than to the sophisticated portraiture of London's best artists. Sargent was to become a better painter later in life, but, clearly, not as the result of his English training.

Figure 92.
Robert Fulton
Benjamin West
Oil on canvas, 1806
91.4 x 71.1 cm. (36 x 28 in.)
The New York State Historical
Association, Cooperstown

Robert Fulton

"One of my adopted sons" was the way Mrs. West referred to Robert Fulton (1765-1815); and her husband, as well, always had a great affection for the man who was to perfect the steamboat. Fulton, a painter from the area of Lancaster, Pennsylvania, came to West at the age of twenty-one in 1786. According to an early biography of the inventor, written by his friend, Cadwallader Colden, in 1817, West took Fulton "into his house, where he continued an inmate for several years."[63] Much later, in 1805, Fulton showed unusual intimacy by sending his mentor a letter headed "My dear Many West" (probably derived from "Benjamin").[64] The next year West painted a rather introspective portrait of his talented young friend [Figure 92], seated next to a window. Through it can be seen a ship struck by one of the torpedoes Fulton had recently designed. Their

Figure 93.
Charles, 3rd Earl Stanhope
Robert Fulton
Oil on canvas, circa 1795
92.1 x 71.7 cm. (36¼ x 28¼ in.)
Henry H. Livingston

close friendship appears to have been about as strong as that which existed between Trumbull and the master.

Nevertheless, it is highly questionable that Fulton actually lived with West. Dunlap gives a more convincing report, that in 1786 "West recommended the apartment I abandoned to Fulton."[65] Dunlap's apartment, a second-story studio with a furnished bedroom above it, was one that West had obtained for him in the Charlotte Street house of Robert Davy, a painter who had been taught in Rome. West was always willing to help find accommodations, and perhaps he even thought that Davy's influence might be beneficial.

Fulton's portrait of *Charles, 3rd Earl Stanhope* [Figure 93], painted about 1795, is his only surviving English work. Lord Stanhope, a rather severe, impetu-

Figure 94.
Joseph Bringhurst
Robert Fulton
Oil on canvas, 1786
62.2 x 47 cm. (24½ x 18½ in.)
Rockwood Museum
(Gordon S. Hargraves), Wilmington

ous man who shared Fulton's interest in steam vessels, is shown holding an engraved plate, implying that he is about to use the printing-press that he had invented. Compared to Fulton's pre-London oils, such as his 1786 *Joseph Bringhurst* [Figure 94], the likeness of Stanhope indicates that he did not change very much other than to use softer lines, purer and warmer colors in the flesh, and paint made more liquid with turpentine. Earlier, his flesh tints were blended to one shade which tended to be somewhat muddy. The most striking difference between the two, the introduction of more color, may well have been urged by West. Fulton seems to have had an interest in meticulous detail, which may have originated in his background as a miniaturist, and in the clever use of light for *trompe-l'oeil* effects, as in the shining printer's plate that Stanhope carried, or in the crisp streak of light illuminating the edge of Bringhurst's coat.

Although, rather mysteriously, Fulton was apparently nearly admitted, and then refused, admission into the Academy schools in 1790,[66] he submitted portraits to the annual exhibitions for 1791 and 1793. He was better represented at the Society of Artists in 1791 where, along with two portraits, he entered two subject pictures: *Elisha Raising the Widow's Son* (a theme also treated by West) and *Priscilla and Alladine, from Spenser's Faërie Queene* (both unlocated). Perhaps on the advice of West, who believed that the survival of history painters depended upon their devising "a scheme" with engravers, Fulton made his trial in 1793 with the sensation of the day, *Louis XVI in Prison Taking Leave of His Family* (painting and engraving unlocated). The tenderness of this famous farewell, before the French king's shocking martyrdom, was perfectly attuned to the sentiment of the period, and it had the additional appeal of topicality since the tragedy had occurred within the year. Mather Brown, among other artists, recognized the salability of this theme, but Fulton decided to create an engraved series by following it with portraits of other royal martyrs. These likenesses are more notable for their beauty than for historical accuracy: *Mary Queen of Scots Under Confinement*, and *Lady Jane Grey the Night Before Her Execution*. The last two pictures survive in the form of mezzotints by James Ward [Figures 95 and 96]. This was Fulton's one effort, apparently not too successful, to branch

(left)
Figure 95.
Mary Queen of Scots Under Confinement
James Ward, after Robert Fulton
Mezzotint, 1793
50.5 x 35.3 cm. (19⅞ x 13⅞ in.)
The Metropolitan Museum of Art, New York, Gift of Miss Georgiana W. Sargent in Memory of John Osborne Sargent, 1924

(right)
Figure 96.
Lady Jane Grey the Night Before Her Execution
James Ward, after Robert Fulton
Mezzotint, 1793
50.5 x 35.3 cm. (19⅞ x 13⅞ in.)
The Metropolitan Museum of Art, New York, Gift of Miss Georgiana W. Sargent in Memory of John Osborne Sargent, 1924

into areas other than portraiture. Finally, to avoid the competition of London, he moved in 1793 to Devonshire, where he practiced as a portrait painter for about a year before completely giving in to the distraction of his scientific interests.

When Reynolds died in February of 1792, West was unanimously elected, at age fifty-four, the second president of the Royal Academy. He was generally popular with other artists and, of course, all knew that he had the strong support of the king. For history painters, the presence of one of their own in this exalted chair seemed a welcome presentiment of a new era. Fulton, who had always admired Benjamin West, was elated. "West is now at the head of his profession," he wrote to a friend in Pennsylvania, "and Presides at the Royal Academy over all the Painters in England—But he is a Great Genius and merits all the honour he has obtained . . . he now looks Round on the beauties of pas[t] Industry—An Ornament to Society and Stimulis to young Men."[67]

Years later, in 1810, with the same fervor, Fulton led an unsuccessful campaign for the Pennsylvania Academy of the Fine Arts to purchase twenty-five of his master's paintings, arguing that *West is the most correct draftsman ever known; That he groups his figures and tells his story well; That he is highly poetical in his compositions and the most clasic painter of the present age; That his works are of so superior a Character as to form, I might say guarantee, a fine taste to our future artists.*[68] His listeners would have agreed to the superlatives, but the price, at seventy-five-hundred pounds, was prohibitive.

This generation's students differed from the last, in that they expected to return to a new country with a government whose artistic aspirations were not yet defined. For those who had vision, such as Trumbull, there was the hope of assuming a position of leadership in a world no longer dependent upon Britain, and in a nation now capable of bringing appropriate glory to her artists. There would, of course, be commissions for pictures of national heroes and for scenes of the splendid military victories of the War of Independence. Fulton, Brown, Raphael West, and Trumbull, and, much later, Sargent and Dunlap, were all history painters, believing completely in the ideal set by the venerated Benjamin West.

Notes

1. Dunlap, *History*, vol. 1, p. 33.

2. *Ibid.*, p. 93; and letter, Mrs. Benjamin West to Mrs. John Trumbull, September 29, 1806, mentions Robert Fulton, "one of my adopted sons" (Stan V. Henkels auction sale catalogue, Philadelphia, June 8, 1917, no. 699).

3. Dunlap, *History*, vol. 1, p. 340.

4. Theodore Sizer, ed., *The Autobiography of Colonel John Trumbull, Patriot-Artist, 1756-1843* (New Haven: 1953), p. 45.

5. *A Catalogue of a Few Finished Original Pictures . . . of the Late Benjamin West, Esq. P.R.A.*, George Robins, auctioneer (London: 1829) June 20-22, 1829; sales no. 123.

6. Letter (copy), William Temple Franklin to William Caslon, April 5, 1781, William Temple Franklin's Letter Book, Library of Congress, Washington, D. C.

7. Letter (typescript copy), Mather Brown to the Byles family, September 10, 1781, Mather Brown's Correspondence, Massachusetts Historical Society, Boston.

8. Letter, Mather Brown to the Byles family, February 24, 1782, Byles Papers, Massachusetts Historical Society, Boston.

9. Wark, *Joshua Reynolds*, pp. 41-42 (Reynolds's Third Discourse, 1770); and Dunlap, *History*, vol. 1, p. 184.

10. Letter, Mather Brown to the Byles family, August 5, 1782, Byles Papers, Massachusetts Historical Society, Boston.

11. Benjamin West, *A Discourse Delivered to the Students of the Royal Academy, (Dec. 10, 1792)* (London: 1793), p. 30.

12. Letter, Mather Brown to the Byles family, August 5, 1782, Byles Papers, Massachusetts Historical Society, Boston.

13. Dunlap, *History*, vol. 1, p. 182.

14. *Ibid.*, p. 185.

15. *Ibid.*

16. Letter, Charles Bulfinch to his mother, September 17, 1786, Harvard University. A typed copy is in the Fogg Art Museum, Cambridge, Massachusetts.

17. Whitley, *Artists*, vol. 2, p. 100.

18. Dunlap, *History*, vol. 1, p. 356.

19. Sizer, *Autobiography of Trumbull*, pp. 86-87.

20. John Trumbull's Correspondence, Sterling Library, Yale University, New Haven, Connecticut.

21. Morgan, *Gilbert Stuart*, p. 84.

22. *Ibid.*

23. Letter, West to Charles Willson Peale, June 15, 1783, on microfilm D23, Robert Graham Collection, Archives of American Art, Washington, D. C.

24. Sizer, *Autobiography of Trumbull*, p. 87.

25. Letter, Trumbull to B. West, August 30, 1790, Sterling Library, Yale University, New Haven, Connecticut.

26. Irma B. Jaffe, *John Trumbull, Patriot-Artist of the American Revolution* (Boston: 1975), p. 324.

27. Theodore Sizer, *The Works of Colonel John Trumbull, Artist of the American Revolution* (New Haven: 1967), p. 135.

28. West believed that composition was his forte (Joseph Farington, *The Farington Diary*, ed. James Greig [London: 1927], entry for January 17, 1797). The best discussions of color are in Franziska Foster-Hahn, "The Sources of True Taste," *Journal of the Warburg and Courtauld Institutes* 30 (1967): 369-71; Groce Evans, *Benjamin West and the Taste of His Times* (Carbondale, Ill.: 1959), pp. 105-7; and Sizer, *Works of Trumbull*, pp. 102-3.

29. Sizer, *Autobiography of Trumbull*, p. 87, n. 11.

30. *Ibid.*, p. 88, n. 15.

31. *Ibid.*, p. 91.

32. Jaffe, *Trumbull*, p. 83. For Poggi, see Sizer, *Autobiography of Trumbull*, p. 90, n. 17.

33. Sizer, *Autobiography of Trumbull*, p. 90, n. 17.

34. "Press Cuttings from English Newspapers on Matters of Artistic Interest, 1686-1835," vol. 2, f. 474, Library of the Victoria and Albert Museum, London.

35. Sir William H. Dillon, *A Narrative of My Professional Adventures (1790-1939)*, ed. Michael A. Lewis (London: 1953), vol. 1, p. 158.

36. "The Late Mather Brown, Esq.," *Library of the Fine Arts*, vol. 1 (London: 1831-32), p. 454.

37. Letter (typescript copy), September 6, 1823, Mather Brown's Correspondence, Massachusetts Historical Society, Boston.

38. Joseph Farington, *Diary*, entry for May 5, 1807. There are a number of landscape drawings at the Pierpont Morgan Library and at the Museum of Fine Arts, Boston, attributed to Benjamin, Jr. Not one is signed.

39. Dunlap, *History*, vol. 2, pt. 1, p. 147.

40. See the diary of Samuel Shoemaker, entry for November 2, 1784, in the Historical Society of Pennsylvania, Philadelphia; and Thomas S. Duché's letter to the Rt. Rev. William White, August 7, 1789, in the Church Historical Society, Austin, Texas.

41. Albert Frank Gegenheimer, "Artist in Exile: The Story of Thomas Spence Duché," *The Pennsylvania Magazine of History and Biography* 79 (January 1955): 9-10.

42. Letter, T.S. Duché to Mrs. John Morgan, June 7, 1783, Historical Society of Pennsylvania, Philadelphia.

43. See Dr. H. Selfe Bennett, "The Story of Two Old Prints," *Art in America*, 1964 reprint of volume 6, 1918, p. 243; Duché's father was chaplain of the asylum for female orphans represented in his son's picture.

44. Letter, John Trumbull to Thomas Jefferson, May 7, 1788, Library of Congress, Washington, D.C.

45. Frederic Fairchild Sherman ("James Earl, a Forgotten American Portrait Painter," *Art in America and Elsewhere* 23, no. 4 [October 1935]: 143) appears to be the earliest source for this idea.

46. Anna Wells Rutledge, *Artists in the Life of Charleston* (Philadelphia: 1949), p. 124.

47. Dunlap, *Diary*, vol. 2, p. 543n; and Dunlap, *History*, vol. 1, p. 427.

48. The documented portrait of *Lady Caroline Beauclerk* appears to be the one, once attributed to an unidentified artist, that the author saw in the collection of the Duke of St. Albans. It has since been sold at Christie's, June 23, 1978, as by Sir Williams Beechey. It is definitely not by Beechey and is very similar to Earl's later known work. With it, in the same sale, went several other possible portraits by Earl having the same provenance.

49. Dunlap, *History*, vol. 1, p. 256.

50. *Ibid.*, p. 243.

51. *Ibid.*, p. 258.

52. *Ibid.*, p. 262.

53. J. Hall Pleasants, "George William West, a Baltimore Student of Benjamin West," *Art in America* 37, no. 1 (January 1949): 9.

54. Dunlap, *History*, vol. 2, pt. 1, p. 58.

55. Letter, the Byles family to Mather Brown, June 15, 1793, Letter Book of Mary and Catherine Byles, May 1793-August 1808, transcript, Massachusetts Historical Society, Boston, where he is referred to as "Mr. Johnson in this town." John Johnston's name was frequently spelled this way; he was the one member of the Johnston family of ornamental painters who practiced as a portraitist in Boston in 1793. The stylistic connection with Sargent is unmistakable.

56. Letter, H. Sargent to Lovett, March 27, 1795, Henry Sargent Papers, Essex Institute, Salem, Mass. Beware of the inaccurate transcript in Julia De Wolfe Addison, "Henry Sargent: A Boston Painter," *Art in America and Elsewhere* 17, no. 6 (October 1929): 279-80.

57. Letter, H. Sargent to William Dunlap, May 5, 1833, Gratz Collection, Historical Society of Pennsylvania, Philadelphia. Samuel Jennings, about whom Dunlap knew so little, may have been one of West's pupils. John Jennings, his father, wrote to West on May 12, 1788, to

thank him for "improving" his son "in the great Art of painting" (Benjamin West Papers, Historical Society of Pennsylvania). The son had arrived in London in July of 1787 with a portrait style reminiscent of Charles Willson Peale. His later known work, *Liberty Displaying the Arts and Sciences*, of 1792, is not close to West's style.

58. Letter, H. Sargent to Lovett, March 27, 1795, Henry Sargent Papers, Essex Institute, Salem, Mass.

59. Letter, H. Sargent to his brother, April 26, 1796, Sargent-Murray-Gilman-Hough House Papers, 1744-1886, Massachusetts Historical Society, Boston.

60. *Ibid.*

61. Dunlap, *History*, vol. 1, p. 260.

62. Letter, H. Sargent to Lovett, March 27, 1795, Henry Sargent Papers, Essex Institute, Salem, Mass.

63. Cadwallader D. Colden, *The Life of Robert Fulton* (New York: 1817), p. 10.

64. Letter, R. Fulton to B. West, October 16, 1805, Robert Fulton Papers, The New-York Historical Society, New York. Cynthia Philip, who is working on a biography of Fulton, first suggested to me that "Many" could be short for "Benjamin."

65. Dunlap, *History*, vol. 1, p. 260.

66. Sidney C. Hutchison, "The Royal Academy Schools, 1768-1830," *The Walpole Society* 38 (1962): 150, 152. Possibly his rejection was related to his absence. He took a short trip (months unknown) to France in 1790.

67. Letter, R. Fulton to David Morris, May 21, 1793, Chicago Historical Society.

68. Letter, R. Fulton to G. Clymer, April 12, 1810, microfilm P63 of The Pennsylvania Academy of the Fine Arts archives, Archives of American Art, Washington, D. C. About half the group of pictures were originals, and the rest were copies, at a price which equaled $32,888.

Last Supper Benjamin West Somerville & Simpson Ltd, London
Page 18

John Coats Browne Joseph Wright The Fine Arts Museums of San Francisco, Gift of Mr. and Mrs. John D. Rockefeller 3rd
Page 51

Henrietta Elizabeth Frederica Vane Gilbert Stuart Smith College Museum of Art, Northampton, Massachusetts, Given in memory of Jessie Rand Goldthwait ('90) by her husband and daughter, 1957

Page 58

The Sortie Made by the Garrison of Gibraltar, November 27, 1781 John Trumbull The Metropolitan Museum of Art, New York; Pauline V. Fullerton Bequest; Mr. and Mrs. James Walter Carter Gift; Mr. and Mrs. Raymond J. Horowitz Gift; Erving Wolf Foundation Gift; Vain and Harry Fish Foundation, Inc.,Gift; Gift of Hanson K. Corning, by exchange; and Maria DeWitt Jesup and Morris K. Jesup Funds, 1976

Page 92

Thomas, Earl of Surrey, Son of John, 1st Duke of Norfolk, Defending His Allegiance to Richard III before Henry VII after the Battle of Bosworth Field, 1485 Mather Brown His Grace the Duke of Norfolk, CB.
Page 97

The Dead Man Restored to Life by Touching the Bones of the Prophet Elisha   Washington Allston
The Pennsylvania Academy of the Fine Arts, Philadelphia

Page 138

Dying Hercules   Samuel F. B. Morse   Yale University Art Gallery, New Haven; Gift of the Artist
Page 164

The Murder of Rutland by Lord Clifford   Charles Robert Leslie   The Pennsylvania Academy of the Fine Arts, Philadelphia
Page 167

THE THIRD GENERATION
1800-1820

This generation of American artists in London was more removed from Benjamin West than the previous ones. He was preoccupied with his own painting and Royal Academy affairs during the first decade of the new century, and his awesome position now made interruption seem to be a greater imposition. Although the newcomers continued to visit "Mr. West," they began to band together outside of his studio, and finally, in 1811, found their natural leader in one of his older American students, Washington Allston. "Every thing about [Allston] bespoke the man of intellect and refinement" is the way his friend Washington Irving described him. "His conversation was copious, animated and highly graphic; warmed by a general sensibility and benevolence and intervened at times by a chaste and gentle humor." If anyone was willing to keep Allston company, he "would sit up until cock crowing, and it was hard to break away from the charms of his conversation."[1] For younger pupils, such as Charles Robert Leslie, he was a pivotal figure, "one of a very few excellent persons I have known in the course of my life, whose rare endowments have rendered it next to impossible that I should 'ever look upon the like again.'" Another follower, the English artist William Collins, recalled that he had "a power of intellect and imagination I never saw surpassed."[2] Allston, like Stuart before him but to a greater extent, adopted some of West's students and exerted the more decisive influence.

Washington Allston

Washington Allston (1779-1843), the son of a South Carolina planter, graduated from Harvard in 1800 as the class poet. He had a burning desire, however, to be a painter. After selling his share of the family property, he sailed to England in May of 1801 with his friend, the accomplished miniaturist, Edward G. Malbone. Allston's painting style and subject matter, at this point, were imitative of a number of different artists, suggesting a lack of direction. While *The Tippler*, dated 1799 (Amherst College), is a seventeenth-century Dutch theme and *Tragic Figure in Chains*, dated 1800 [Figure 97], embodies the horror of Henry Fuseli's subjects in contemporary engravings, both pictures are highly detailed in contrast to the loosely suggestive style of *A Rocky Coast with Banditti* [Figure 98], dated 1800. The style, not yet his own, was adapted to the subject matter; but in portraiture he was more consistent, less imitative, and particularly concerned with color, as in his early *Self-Portrait* [Figure 99]. Revealing the highest ambitions, he even attempted history, with his heads of *Peter Hearing the*

Figure 97.
Tragic Figure in Chains
Washington Allston
Oil on canvas, 1800
31.4 x 24.1 cm. (12⅜ x 9½ in.)
Addison Gallery of American Art,
Phillips Academy,
Andover, Massachusetts
Not in exhibition

Cock Crow and *Judas Iscariot* (both unlocated), where the emphasis would have been on emotional facial expression.

On proof of his ability to draw from plaster casts, Allston was accepted into the Royal Academy schools in October of 1801. Although no securely dated London work is known to survive,[3] his exhibited pieces at the Royal Academy (spring of 1802 and 1803) are evidence of a continuation of his American proclivities. He entered two landscapes with bandits in 1802, one of which had been painted at Harvard, and a comical *French Soldier Telling a Story* (unlocated). "I did not get rid of this banditti mania," he later recounted, "until I had been over a year in England."[4] Banditti subjects are typical of the seventeenth-century

133

Figure 98.
A Rocky Coast with Banditti
Washington Allston
Oil on canvas, 1800
34.9 x 48.2 cm. (13¾ x 19 in.)
Museum of Early Southern Decorative Arts, Winston-Salem, North Carolina

Italian Salvator Rosa, whose pictures were very popular in eighteenth-century England; and, in fact, what is thought to be Allston's earliest work abroad, a fanciful *Landscape* [Figure 100] with anecdotal figures in the foreground, is basically Salvatoresque and probably dates about 1803. As in banditti pictures, the figures are Italian peasants of an earlier period, adding a picturesque element of nostalgia. While exposing his lack of training in the impossible anatomy of the washerwoman, the artist also shows that he has learned, from earlier landscapists such as Rosa, how to use alternating dark and light zones from foreground to middle ground to distance as a means of measuring receding space.

Allston left America "strongly prejudiced," as he said, against West, who was sixty-three and had led the Academy for nine years. The few prints he had seen from his work were not special, but, once in London, Allston soon found that he admired West more than he had expected. An early letter, of August 1801, to a friend in Charleston states: "You will no doubt be surprised that among the many painters in London I should rank M\ West as the first." He had once judged him unimaginative, but *no fancy could have better concieved and no pencil more happily embodied the visions of sublimity, than he has in his inimitable picture from Revelation . . . a more sublime and awful picture I never beheld . . . and I am certain no painter has exceeded M\ West in the fury horror and despair which he has represented.* He thought that other pictures (unnamed) in West's gallery were "of similar merit." But it is significant that *Death on a Pale Horse* (probably the 1796 Petworth version [Figure 101]) should have caught his eye; showing the holocaust described in Revelation 6, following the opening of the four seals, it is West's most wildly emotional work and one of his best in terms of color.⁵ Later, Allston developed a special appreciation for West's portrayal of character and, in 1841, even pronounced several heads in West's *Christ Rejected by the Jews* [Figure 6] "equal to Raphael. Nothing can surpass the High Priest and many others."⁶

As described by Washington Irving, Allston, in 1805, was especially "moved and roused by objects of grandeur," and he "took great delight in paintings which excelled in colour."⁷ With this particular sensitivity, it is no wonder that Allston set about to learn the English technique of dead coloring with underpaint in a hue quite different from the end result, and then building upon this with thin glazes of transparent color until the desired shade was reached, but with a greater resonance than with the direct application of mixed color. Allston's use of glazing

Figure 99.
Self-Portrait
Washington Allston
Oil on canvas, 1796/1800
83.8 x 66 cm. (33 x 26 in.)
Fogg Art Museum, Harvard University, Cambridge, Massachusetts
Not in exhibition

Figure 100.
Landscape
Washington Allston
Oil on canvas, circa 1803
71.1 x 95.2 cm. (28 x 37½ in.)
Private collection

so distinguished him from his contemporaries that he was called "the American Titian" when he visited the Continent in 1803-8. To compliments on the deep richness of his effects, he replied that he had acquired his technique in England.[8] Glazing and painting into successive glazes was an almost universal practice among the London artists. Reynolds's technique of multilayers, sometimes introducing wax and varnish into the glazes, with many reworkings, was one of the most elaborate; and Allston later deeply regretted that he had arrived in London after his death. He had read Reynolds's published *Discourses* in America and had "always" held him in high esteem. Both artists strove, through experimentation, to recapture the spirit of the Old Masters, and both had a tendency to belabor their pictures so that as many as ten different versions might exist below the surface.[9]

West was of special help to Allston in advising him on his entrance-drawings for the Royal Academy, and in encouraging him when other artists, such as Fuseli, told him that if he wanted to be a history painter he had better be prepared to starve. Fuseli, however, was known for his acridity, and once even told young Stuart that he would be more successful as a cobbler.[10] But, with West to take "me by the hand," Allston was not discouraged. "His gallery was open to me at all times, and his advice always ready and kindly given," reported Allston, for "he was a man overflowing with the milk of human kindness."[11] Before Allston even applied for admission to the Academy in 1801, he made a second attempt "that will far surpass anything I have done before" on the theme of Peter's denial of Christ, but with full-length figures two feet high.[12] Possibly this missing picture was inspired by West's huge scriptural canvases, for most of West's work now was Biblical.

In any case, we can be more sure of West's influence during Allston's second period in London, from 1811 to 1818. His decision then to concentrate on religious subject matter on a large scale was almost certainly the result of West's celebrated example. Another student, C.R. Leslie, as much as says this: "Encouraged by the success West had met in exhibiting large pictures from sacred history [at the Royal Academy and recently at the British Institution], Allston contemplated an exhibition of [*The Dead Man Restored*], and when near its completion he hired a room for this purpose, in Pall Mall."[13]

The Dead Man Restored to Life by Touching the Bones of the Prophet Elisha [Figure 102; color, page 129] was displayed in a one-man show for a few days, and then, at the urging of his friends, Allston changed his mind and sent it to the annual exhibition given in the winter of 1814 at the British Institution. Organized to supplement the Academy's shows and to boost British patronage in areas other than portraiture, the British Institution offered a prize of two-hundred guineas for the best entry. When Allston won this award, his future as a history painter seemed to be assured, but with a kind of picture that was quite different from the reportage paintings of Trumbull and Brown. There is a greater emotional force in Allston, not only because of the spiritual significance of his subjects but also because of an intensity in his figure-drawing, which one critic aptly described as "a

Figure 101.
Death on a Pale Horse
Benjamin West
Oil on canvas, 1796
58.4 x 128.3 cm. (23½ x 50½ in.)
The Detroit Institute of Arts, the Robert H. Tannahill Foundation Fund, American Colonial and Federal Art

Figure 102.
The Dead Man Restored to Life by Touching the Bones of the Prophet Elisha
Washington Allston
Oil on canvas, 1811–14
396.2 x 304.8 cm. (156 x 120 in.)
The Pennsylvania Academy of the Fine Arts, Philadelphia
Not in Washington

sort of artificial heat . . . much as if it were latent, elaborated with great care."[14] Unlike Trumbull and Brown, Allston distilled his style, while in Italy, from antique sculpture and the Old Masters, most especially Titian and Michelangelo. In this way he conformed to Reynolds's dictate that the models should not be living artists.[15] West's reaction (which pleased Allston), when he saw *The Dead Man Restored* in Allston's studio, was that it was "of the fifteenth century"; and it reminded one discerning collector, Sir George Beaumont, of the sixteenth-century work of Sebastiano del Piombo.[16] Although the painting gives the impression of having been constructed piecemeal, with much academic study of anatomy and emotional expression, the gesture of the awakening dead man was one of Allston's

138

most effective emotive devices. One newspaper critic pronounced the picture "the most perfect and Titianesque piece of art of modern times."[17]

The Dead Man Restored was not painted to be engraved, in the tradition of Trumbull and Brown's work, but rather as an exhibition piece which might be sold. It was well known that the British Institution had paid three thousand guineas, in 1811, for West's *Christ Healing the Sick in the Temple*, the largest sum ever spent for a modern work. Furthermore, despite the fact that West's thirty-five paintings for the Revealed Religion series at Windsor were left as an incomplete project, he had so built his reputation by exhibiting these pictures at the Academy, along with those painted for William Beckford's Fonthill Abbey, that he stimulated a new interest in Biblical subjects on the part of other artists and, to a limited extent, patrons. One such patron was Sir George Beaumont, who admired the unfinished canvas for *The Dead Man Restored* in Allston's studio so much that, in 1812, he commissioned a scriptural subject (which became *The Angel Releasing St. Peter from Prison* [Figure 103]). This was intended for a parish church which he had constructed near his country seat in Ashby-de-la-Zouch, Leicestershire. Such commissions were still unusual and, although *The Dead Man Restored* enhanced Allston's reputation, it was not easy to find a buyer for such large historical pieces.

Allston was not specifically, not provably, indebted to West other than for subject matter and inspiring example. In fact, most of his religious themes had already been treated by West, such as *The Angel Releasing St. Peter*, *Christ Healing the Sick*, *Belshazzar's Feast*, *Saul and the Witch of Endor*, *The Angel and the Three Marys*, *The Angel of Wrath*, and *Uriel in the Sun* which is comparable to West's *Angel in the Sun*. He probably asked West's advice on any number of occasions because he had great respect for his experience, and, as he later told Dunlap, West was "more than a father to him."[18] Allston believed, for instance, that West was "one of the most learned in Europe" when it came to problems of connoisseurship and attribution. In 1815, when Allston wanted an expert opinion on a picture that he had bought—supposedly by Veronese—West was the one man to approach; and his conclusion that it was an old Venetian copy was accepted without question.[19] As Lord Lonsdale confided to the landscapist Joseph Farington over dinner one evening in 1813, "West . . . had a great deal of information," and "if the manner in which [he] expresses His information was better than it is He would be justly estimated much more highly than He now is."[20] Allston, who was more intellectual than West, valued his extensive practical knowledge; and such was his admiration that, in his surviving recollections of the man, it never occurred to him to mention any awkwardness of expression.

Always conscious of West's work as a precedent, Allston deliberately strove not to be an imitator. In 1813, he made preliminary sketches for a *Christ Healing the Sick* (Fogg Art Museum and Worcester Art Museum), with the object of showing, as in *The Dead Man Restored*, the enactment of a miracle. Since the subject had already been portrayed "so admirably," as Allston thought, by West, he was careful to choose a different moment; but he finally abandoned the project as unsuccessful.[21]

Figure 103.
*The Angel Releasing St. Peter
from Prison*
Washington Allston
Oil on canvas, 1814–16
316.2 x 275.6 cm. (124½ x 108½ in.)
Museum of Fine Arts, Boston,
Gift of Robert William Hooper
Not in exhibition

In the case of *The Angel Releasing St. Peter from Prison*, which was Beaumont's commission for his parish church, Allston remarked to Leslie that he thought he could prove that West was mistaken in one of his more recent rules for executing a background. He had found it expedient to wash in this area with umber, which, according to West, would be too deadening: "If you once lose the ground of your canvas in the background, it is not within the reach of art to supply the loss."[22] After one abortive attempt which seemed to support West's argument, Allston was delighted to find that he could still produce an effect of transparency by over-glazing the dark brown with pure primary colors. Considering the use of glazing in this painting, it is perhaps no wonder that it was not finished until 1816. Peter's cloak, for instance, is a composite of bluish-brown painted over vermilion, still visible through the cracks. The head of Peter, so dramatically expressive, is the closest Allston came to West's contemporary work.

Despite his breadth of exposure, Allston was essentially English-trained, and he liked to be associated with this part of his background. From Boston in 1819, he announced, "I shall hope to preserve my claims as one of the British School," and, in 1840, he wrote to the editor of the *North American Review*: "I owe much of whatever knowledge I may possess of my art to the English school; my connexion with which,—and no less from respect than affection,—I shall ever hold in high value."[23] His loyalty was partly due to the warmth of his friendships in England, but he also received special recognition from the Royal Academy by being elected an Associate member in 1818, just after leaving for America.

Allston's English background is reflected as well in his *Lectures on Art*, written chiefly in the 1830s, where he asserts that the education of an artist involves the development of his "moral being."[24] The concept does not originate with West, but it became one of his strongest themes. In the same way, when Allston had to defend the proportions of two of his figures in *The Dead Man Restored* in 1826, he fell back on an argument which is typical of West: "It is grounded on a sound principle extracted from the study of the antique and the old masters, particularly the latter. Michael Angelo owes much of his grandeur to this principle."[25] Thus, on a more intangible, even subconscious level, Allston was affected by the outlook of his teacher.

West's few discourses, as president of the Royal Academy, followed along the lines of his distinguished predecessor but were less intellectual and, as his contemporaries seemed to agree, were marked by "plain practical sense."[26] He differed from Reynolds in his constant plea for patronage, usually with the enticement of emphasizing the moral and commercial uses of art or the immortality that it would bring to patrons.[27] Instead of establishing a set of principles for upgrading the quality of contemporary art, as Reynolds had already done, West tried to use his position for the financial benefit of all artists. He spurred potential patrons by reminding them of the obligations of patriotism: "By collecting from other countries, [the patron] may greatly enrich himself, but can never give celebrity to the country in which he lives."[28] At another time, he urged that drawing be "taught as an elementary essential in education," which, of course, would mean more openings for drawing-masters.²⁹

The second major theme in West's discourses, for the benefit of young artists, was "the indispensable necessity of virtuous principles and of a virtuous life" and the need for using the arts in the "service of truth, justice, honor, and the love of our country."³⁰ This was not only an attempt to improve the image of the profession, but a reflection of the way West saw himself. He was known for the "pious choice" of his subjects, and went so far as to claim that "the works of Raphael and Michael Angelo, considered without reference to the manifestations which they exhibit of moral influence, possess no merit beyond the productions of the ordinary paper-hanger."³¹ In 1809, West wrote to his former pupil, Charles Willson Peale, in regard to Peale's son, Rembrandt, who intended to expand his father's series of portraits of famous men, exhibited for profit in Philadelphia: *Although I am friendly to portraying eminent men, I am not friendly to the indiscrimanate waste of genius in Portrait Painting—and I hope your Son will ever bear in his Mind, that the Art of painting has powers to dignify man, by transmitting to posterity his noble actions . . . to be viewed in those invaluable lessons of religion, love of country, and morality.*³²

Rembrandt Peale

Rembrandt Peale (1778-1860) was himself one of West's erstwhile students. As the son of a scientist-cum-painter, he came to London in 1802 with his younger brother, Rubens, and a mastodon skeleton which his father had unearthed in upper New York State. Rubens was meant to exhibit the prehistoric curiosity as the means of the brothers' support while Rembrandt improved as an artist. Despite the fact that Rembrandt had already proven his professional talent with even a skillfully painted life-portrait of *George Washington* (Historical Society of Pennsylvania), it was hoped that he would strengthen his resources under Benjamin West and the professors at the Royal Academy. West received the rather conceited Rembrandt with the affection he felt for the elder Peale, introduced him to Allston and the English portrait painter Thomas Lawrence, and supervised his studies in his gallery; but, after the young man, who signed his work without his surname, had sketched for a while from the casts at the Royal Academy, he was refused admission to the life class—in other words, official enrollment—because of an undescribed "trick practiced on Mr. West."³³ According to his own account, however, he accomplished at least two likenesses of prominent men for his father's exhibition gallery, the Peale Museum in Philadelphia. The poet Robert Bloomfield, "whom I taught to draw," and Sir Joseph Banks had apparently agreed to sit on request.³⁴ Rembrandt also sent two portraits to the Royal Academy in 1803, an anonymous one in chalk and another of himself holding a tooth from the mastodon, before returning to his father.

The only surviving work is the portrait of *Sir Joseph Banks* [Figure 104], a distinguished naturalist, which is much freer in treatment than the pre-London, 1801 portrait of *Rubens Peale with a Geranium* [Figure 105]. With elaborate penciling around the eyes, eyebrows, and mouth, and squiggles of viscous paint in the hair, Rembrandt's later portrait evinces an indulgence, which was rare for him, in effects of technique. This was a passing phase, undoubtedly inspired by contemporary English painting.

Figure 104.
Sir Joseph Banks
Rembrandt Peale
Oil on canvas, probably 1802
59.7 x 49.5 cm. (23½ x 19½ in.)
The Academy of Natural Sciences
of Philadelphia

Figure 105.
Rubens Peale with a Geranium
Rembrandt Peale
Oil on canvas, 1801
71.1 x 61 cm. (28 x 24 in.)
Mrs. Norman B. Woolworth
Not in exhibition

Figure 106.
Benjamin West
Abraham G. D. Tuthill
Oil on panel, circa 1840
57.1 x 48.2 cm. (22½ x 19 in.)
Mrs. Stewart Taft Beach

Abraham G. D. Tuthill

Two other pupils who appear to have been little affected by West were Abraham G. D. Tuthill (1776-1843) from Long Island, New York, who was in London in 1800, and Edward G. Malbone from Newport, Rhode Island, who was there briefly in 1801. Tuthill's friends and patrons, pleased with his early portraits, offered to sponsor his further education, and so it was decided in 1799 that he would study under Gilbert Stuart in Philadelphia. Stuart did not welcome the idea of an apprentice, for that was what was evidently intended, and produced the most extraordinary excuse that he "is going within the term of two months to join the English army at Canada and from thence he goes to London, therefor it would not be in his power to give any information in respect to painting." Of course, Stuart made no such move, but he did advise Tuthill "to go to England to get my education under the tuition of M[r] West."[35] Hence, after a couple of months in France, Tuthill appeared in London by early August of 1800. The story that he was in England for about seven years before spending a year in France goes back to at least 1882 with nothing to contradict it. But he was in New York by 1808, where Dunlap, meeting him about two years later, reported that his work "bore little indication" that the artist had been schooled in London, although he "claimed to be a pupil of Mr. West's."[36]

Until now, three of Tuthill's known paintings have been published as his English work, but actually it is much more likely that all were produced in America.[37] The two portraits on panel of *Benjamin West*, once thought to have been from life, were copied from an 1804 mezzotint after Andrew Robertson's miniature of *Benjamin West*, in which he is shown, nearly full-face, holding a scroll. One version (Shelburne Museum) by Tuthill includes this accessory which was eliminated in the other copy [Figure 106]. The pigments in both panels, rather somber and almost monochromatic, are closest to Tuthill's late pictures of around 1840. The third painting, a large *Nativity* (Mrs. H. England, Montpelier, Vt.), is also not consistent with Tuthill's early style, either just before or just after his stay in England.[38] His work, on returning to the United States, suggests that he, like Rembrandt Peale in 1808, was especially susceptible to the French neoclassical preference for convincing deception at the expense of an English indulgence in richness of paint texture and color.

Malbone (1777-1807), who stayed in London for about five months, from June through October 1801, as Allston's somewhat older traveling companion, found West "decidedly the greatest painter amongst them for history." Furthermore, as Malbone wrote home elatedly, *Mr. West has complimented Mr. Allston and myself, and tells us we shall excel in the art. Yesterday was the first time he had seen a picture of my painting; to-day he condescended to walk a mile to pay me a visit, and told me that I must not look forward to any thing short of the highest excellence.*[39] The picture that had occasioned West's visit was Malbone's handsome miniature likeness of *Washington Allston* [Figure 107], which had evidently been painted in the same year. Allston's contemporary account of the same episode gives West's first reaction on seeing the miniature: "'I have seldom,' said he, 'seen a miniature that pleased me more.'"[40] Indeed, in the strength of the likeness as well as the sensitive nuances of color, it is remarkably fine. Malbone, in 1801, was not only well established professionally but was generally recognized as the best miniaturist in the United States.[41]

Malbone drew at the Royal Academy in the autumn of 1801, but, unlike Allston, he was never enrolled as a student. As he and Allston looked at picture collections in London, it soon became apparent that their attitudes were quite different. According to Allston's descendant and biographer, Jared B. Flagg, Malbone preferred the work of contemporary artists, such as Thomas Lawrence,

Edward G. Malbone

Figure 107.
Washington Allston
Edward G. Malbone
Watercolor on ivory, 1801
8.9 x 6.9 cm. (3½ x 2¾ in.)
Museum of Fine Arts, Boston,
Charles Henry Hayden Fund
Not in exhibition

(left)
Figure 108.
The Hours
Samuel Shelley
Watercolor on ivory, before 1801
14 x 10.8 cm. (5½ x 4¼ in.)
The Metropolitan Museum of Art,
New York, Bequest of
Collis P. Huntington, 1948
Not in exhibition

(right)
Figure 109.
The Hours
Edward G. Malbone
Watercolor on ivory, 1801
18.4 x 15.4 cm. (7¼ x 6 1/16 in.)
The Providence Athenaeum

Figure 110.
Colonel Thomas Pinckney, Jr.
Edward G. Malbone
Watercolor on ivory, 1802
7.6 x 5.9 cm. (3 x 2 5/16 in.)
Carolina Art Association/Gibbes
Art Gallery, Charleston

to the Old Masters.[42] Rather than to study, it seems that Malbone visited London chiefly to measure his ability against his English contemporaries. In the same letter in which he mentioned West, he ranked Samuel Shelley and Richard Cosway as the top English miniaturists of his day. A group miniature by Shelley [Figure 108] was, in fact, the source for Malbone's miniature allegory of *The Hours* [Figure 109], signed and dated August 1801. The three women portrayed represent the Present, Past, and Future. Malbone's copy, a little over an inch wider in both directions, improves upon Shelley's by enlarging the space surrounding the women and introducing a mysterious, ethereal effect not in the original, by elongating the face and heavily shading the eyes of the central figure who symbolizes the Present. An additional swath of drapery supports the bosom of this figure and acts as a more effective design element than Shelley's thin string of pearls, while the head of the left figure, the Past, is given a more classical profile.

Comparing Malbone's *Washington Allston* with his miniature of *Colonel Thomas Pinckney, Jr.* [Figure 110], painted upon his return to Charleston, one realizes that Malbone's style changed little, if at all, as the result of his London trip. Nevertheless, his business sense and confidence increased considerably. Back in America, the high duty on his luggage suggests that he had stocked up on artists' supplies in London; and his almost immediate acquisition of an account book lends support to the theory that he anticipated a surge in business. Actually, his first five months in Charleston were the most productive in his career, but this is partly because, as he expected, the demand for his work had been piling up during his absence. With a new awareness of his ability, his prices were raised to fifty dollars for a miniature portrait, without a frame, from the thirty-five to forty dollars, possibly with frame, that he had been used to charging in New York in 1800-1.[43]

The next three American students appeared during Allston's absence, and continued the tradition of a development which was relatively independent of West. The aging artist, bordering on seventy, encouraged this sort of initiative on the part of Charles Bird King, Samuel Lovett Waldo, and Thomas Sully. "If you will consult your own mind, you will draw forth a style and character of your own" was one of West's sage pieces of advice. And, on another occasion, he said of an old copy: "But fine as it is admitted to be, we must say, as a borrowed idea, it lessens the merit of the artist's originality of mind."[44]

Charles Bird King

Charles Bird King (1785-1862) came to West probably in 1806, possibly because he had just finished a five-year apprenticeship with Edward Savage in New York, a man who was still reaping some benefit from his three-year London stint (1791-94), where he had learned to engrave on copper and to develop his opportunities as a showman. King also knew two other precursors, Allston and Malbone, from school days in Newport, Rhode Island. He may even have carried a letter of introduction from Malbone, then in Newport, to West. Until fairly recently, Dunlap's statement that King traveled to England in 1805 was accepted as fact, but, according to Malbone's account book, the miniature painter "Sent to London by Mr. Charles King for Ivory" on June 4, 1806, which would imply that King left in that year.[45]

Charles Bird King provided a link between a few of West's pupils. At first,

Figure 111.
Telemachus and Calypso
Benjamin West
Oil on canvas, probably 1806
104.8 x 149.2 cm. (41¼ x 58¾ in.)
Corcoran Gallery of Art,
Washington, D.C.

he shared a room for several months in Titchfield Street with Waldo, two years younger, who had abandoned his practice as a beginning portraitist in Charleston, South Carolina, to seek guidance in London. They both received the private advice of the American president of the Royal Academy and joined the ranks of those drawing from the casts in the Academy's school. When the best of these sketches were submitted on January 21, 1808, for student admittance, King and Waldo were accepted along with twenty-three others, although King's name, through some apparent oversight, was never inscribed in the official register.

The titles of some of King's missing English pictures, preserved through contemporary accounts, suggest that he devoted his stay in London, of about six years, chiefly to making copies. Although he was evidently not as ambitious as his American colleagues, we know that he also experimented in subject matter other than portraits. He left a picture, for instance, of *Lear and Cordelia* along with a *Boy Stealing Fruit from His Sister* with his landlady, but saved for display in America a painting which has been identified as *Children and Bubble* (all unlocated). This last was entered in the 1813 exhibition at the Pennsylvania Academy of the Fine Arts with the caption: "Philosophers like children sometimes choose / To chase the bubble and the substance lose." Such moralizing was to become fairly typical of King, and might well have been encouraged by the new recognition that Hogarth's work was receiving in England.

Figure 112.
Still Life, Game
Charles Bird King
Oil on canvas, 1806
35.6 x 27.9 cm. (14 x 11 in.)
IBM Corporation, Armonk, New York

Two of King's paintings from the English period can be located. One is a copy (Private Collection) from Benjamin West's *Telemachus and Calypso*, probably a version of about 1806 [Figure 111]. A large romantic landscape inspired by Homer's *Odyssey*, it shows the first meeting between Ulysses's son, Telemachus, and Calypso, the queen of the island upon which he is shipwrecked.[46] Strangely enough, the other English painting is an 1806 *Still Life, Game* [Figure 112], completed within a year of his arrival. The subject might be considered highly unusual as the production of a student under West's guidance, but the old master admired excellence, as two of his learned contemporaries agreed, "in every stile of painting";[47] and this is certainly borne out by his taste in collecting, which included a pen-and-ink study of *Dead Game* by Frans Snyders and *A Dead Hare and Other Game* in a landscape by Weenix (probably Jan Baptist Weenix). King could easily have been inspired by the seventeenth-century Dutch still-lifes in the collections and auction-houses of London, as well as the copies after them, and small works in the same vein by such English artists as Benjamin Blake. The subject might have been chosen because the bird theme would be a play on his own middle name; but there was also the attraction of working from still-life which, like an immovable plaster cast, lends itself to a lengthy study of light and form. It would have been an especially attractive challenge for a beginner. Clearly, King was very concerned with composition and textural contrast, as well as the subtle interplay of light hitting the differently colored, soft feathers and culminating in the pearly richness of the white goosander in the center.

The chronological leap from King's early likeness of *Dr. David King*, of about 1800/5 [Figure 113], to what is considered King's next datable portrait, the *Self-Portrait* of 1815 [Figure 114], encompasses not only his whole English

Figure 113.
Dr. David King
Charles Bird King
Oil on canvas, circa 1800/5
76.2 x 63.5 cm. (30 x 25 in.) sight
Redwood Library and Athenaeum, Newport

Figure 114.
Self-Portrait
Charles Bird King
Oil on canvas, 1815
76.2 x 63.5 cm. (30 x 25 in.)
Redwood Library and Athenaeum,
Newport

experience but several years afterward. The handsomely finished *Self-Portrait*, executed in Baltimore, is a remarkable improvement over the awkward *David King*, in the manner of Edward Savage, but the strides made here are not necessarily a reflection of what was learned in England. Rembrandt Peale, also in Baltimore, was to become a major influence, and one feels his presence already in the sharply modeled *Self-Portrait*. Comparing the English *Still-Life, Game* with the pre-London *David King*, it is apparent that King had advanced rapidly, by 1806, in his ability to draw and in his careful observation of light. This improvement may or may not have been partially accomplished in America, but it is most likely that the experience of working in England, a country whose artists were known for sensitivity to color, at least heightened his perception. Leslie, who met King in England in 1811, decided that his "greatest excellence is in his colouring of flesh."[48] A new awareness of color, not evident in the *David King*, can be seen in the delicate glazing of his small and unpretentious *Still-Life*.

Thomas Sully

When Thomas Sully (1783-1872) arrived in July of 1809, supported by seven generous Philadelphians who had subscribed in advance for a copy each "from some excellent picture in London," he delivered letters of introduction, not only to West and others, but to Charles Bird King whom he found living in a boardinghouse at 8 Buckingham Place, Fitzroy Square.[49] King had moved there in 1808, and spent the first nine months sleeping on the floor. The widowed landlady, Mrs. Bridgen, was shocked, but King genially responded that he wanted to be able to claim that "he slept on a board and lived on potatoes while pursuing his studies."[50] He was evidently dependent upon a careful use of his inheritance, but the Spartan life seems to have suited him. At Sully's naive confession that he had hoped to live for three years on four-hundred dollars, King announced that it would last less than three months. "Can you live low?" he asked, taking up the vision of Sully's new poverty with relish. "All I want is bread and water," came the stoical reply. King was so delighted that they combined forces, according to Dunlap's narrative, to "live luxuriously" on Sully's menu augmented by potatoes and milk, in one bedroom and a painting room.[51]

On entering the Newman Street studio for the first time, Sully expected "the famous Mr. West" to be at least six feet tall. Thus, it was with "a momentary disappointment" that he finally beheld the American patriarch. Now over seventy, West was "a little old man."[52] He was then at work on his *Christ Healing the Sick in the Temple*, which was intended as a gift for the Pennsylvania Hospital in Philadelphia. Despite his age, his output continued to be prodigious and of such quality that the review of the last Royal Academy exhibition in *The Morning Herald* (May 2, 1809) found that West towered over competition as a historical painter "like Polyphemous rising among Sicilian swains . . . the fire of his imagination has not been subdued by time, but even burns more vivid than usual."

As an example of his work, Sully brought West a painting he had done of King's head (unlocated). West gently criticized the drawing of the bone structure as too indecisive, and suggested that he study osteology. On this advice, with King, Sully hired a model (the porter at the Academy) to pose in their studio, and he spent his evenings copying anatomical engravings by candlelight. For the rest of his nine months in London, he was occupied chiefly in obtaining copies of paintings in West's collection to fulfill his end of the Philadelphia bargain. He returned to West's studio repeatedly, not only to borrow pictures but to discuss what grounds the Old Masters might have used so that the copies could be as exact as possible. The young painter was most interested, as his notes show, in learning about the effects that result from using different grounds, glazes, and varnishes.[53] During one visit to Newman Street, Sully watched West painting his *Omnia Vincit Amor* (Metropolitan Museum of Art) and nearly sat on a macaw wing on a nearby sofa. This was the basis for the wings of the genii in the picture, West explained, for "I never paint without having the object before me, if it is to be had."[54] Sully never forgot the lesson.

The first painting Sully chose to copy [Figure 115] appears to have been his instructor's *Pylades and Orestes*, of 1766, rather than some of the European pictures in West's collection. The scene shows the moment when Iphigenia, captive priestess of a temple of Artemis, realizes that the two young men brought

(above)
Figure 115.
Pylades and Orestes
Thomas Sully, after Benjamin West
Oil on canvas, 1809
99.2 x 127 cm. (39 1/16 x 50 in.)
James Ricau

(right)
Figure 116.
Stoke Park, Sir Edward Coke's Column
Thomas Sully
Oil on canvas, 1809
55.2 x 85.8 cm. (21 3/4 x 33 3/4 in.)
The Historical Society of Pennsylvania, Philadelphia

Figure 118.
Bandit Taking Up His Post
John Hamilton Mortimer
Oil on panel, date unknown
35.5 x 25.7 cm. (14 x 10⅛ in.)
The Detroit Institute of Arts,
Purchased, Director's Discretionary
Fund
Not in exhibition

Figure 117.
*William B. Wood as
"Charles de Moor"*
Thomas Sully
Oil on canvas, 1811
107.3 x 76.5 cm. (42¼ x 30⅛ in.)
Corcoran Gallery of Art,
Washington, D.C.

to her for sacrifice are Orestes, her brother, and Pylades, her cousin. One of Sully's other attempts (unlocated) was from West's *Telemachus and Calypso*. Since he borrowed these pictures to duplicate in his own painting room, King's copies of both—of which the *Telemachus* survives—were probably done at the same time.

Sully seems to have believed then, as he did six years later, that it is more profitable to learn from living artists than from dead ones.[55] He sought West's instruction, but West, who rarely painted portraits himself, advised him to com-

Figure 119.
Self-Portrait
Thomas Sully
Oil on canvas, 1809
52.1 x 36.8 cm. (20½ x 14½ in.)
Amherst College, Mead Art Museum,
Massachusetts

pare the work of contemporary portraitists and chose his instructor from among them.[56] Thomas Lawrence was then the leading portrait painter, and his work appealed to Sully despite the fact that his pictures appeared "too much loaded with paint, and the red and yellow overpowering."[57] Sully was still very much under the influence of Gilbert Stuart, with whom he had spent about three weeks in Boston in 1807. Thus, although Lawrence gave him lessons, Sully's work, on his return to Philadelphia, and his summation that "English taste is in favour of strong effects, & brilliant colouring" was not altogether sympathetic.[58] It was not until some years later that his portraits fell under the spell of Lawrence's more dramatic form, becoming more glamorous and sensitive to mood.

Sully's conclusion, after nine months, that he had made little progress in portraiture—"except that he had more of the theory" and "his general knowledge of his art was much greater"[59]—was understandably due to the fact that so much of his time was taken up with evening study under Fuseli in the Royal Academy's Antique School, as well as with making copies from historical pictures, and executing his one commission, from John Coates of Philadelphia, for four landscape copies (unlocated). It was while working on these landscapes that he apparently began his larger picture, *Stoke Park, Sir Edward Coke's Column* [Figure 116], inscribed "London Nov. 1809," which is within the conservative English topographical tradition. Sully had been broadened by his experimentation in subject matter other than portraits; not long after his arrival in Philadelphia, he began a

Figure 120.
Fielding Lucas
Thomas Sully
Oil on canvas, circa 1808
66.1 x 53.3 cm. (26 x 21 in.)
The Baltimore Museum of Art, Gift
of a Group of Friends of the Museum

drawing (unlocated), in July of 1810, for an oil painting of *William B. Wood as "Charles de Moor"* [Figure 117] in Joseph Holman's adaptation of Friedrich Schiller's *The Robbers*. Although Wood was evidently done from life, the composition is strongly reminiscent of John Hamilton Mortimer's *Bandit Taking Up His Post* [Figure 118], engraved in 1778, which could well have been part of Sully's recently expanded visual subconscious.

Charles Willson Peale, who was most eager to see the results of Sully's tutelage abroad, soon reported, "I find he is considerably mended in his drawing—some of his pictures are well coloured."[60] Perhaps Sully's greatest advance was made through his anatomical studies, but he had also developed a new concern for poses, the distribution of the drapery, and accessories: in short, the total effect of the picture. Stylistically, the broad, rough treatment of his *Self-Portrait* [Figure 119], painted virtually on the eve of his departure for London, and the free sketchiness of his 1808 *Fielding Lucas* [Figure 120] provide a sharp contrast

155

Figure 121.
Joseph Dugan
Thomas Sully
Oil on canvas, 1810
91.7 x 73.6 cm. (36⅛ x 29 in.)
National Gallery of Art,
Washington, D.C.,
Gift of Herbert L. Pratt, 1945

Samuel Lovett Waldo

with the softer transitions and greater finish of his post-London *oeuvre*, as in his *Joseph Dugan* [Figure 121], completed in 1810, shortly after his return. With the recognition of his new sophistication, of course, came a corresponding increase in prices. A bust-length, for instance, was now sixty dollars or more, instead of fifty dollars.[61]

King's first roommate, Samuel L. Waldo (1783-1861), from Connecticut, not only enrolled at the Royal Academy but succeeded in entering a portrait of a *Mr. M'Dougle* (unlocated) in the annual 1808 exhibition. Writing to his friend, John Trumbull, in 1806, he expressed pleasure that he had been "highly favored with the friendly instruction of M^r. West, whom I sincerely venerate & esteem.

I feel myself almost incompetent," he added, "even to begin the first rudiments of the art in presence of so great an Artist."[62]

Although Waldo limned some portraits at five guineas each, the identities of the sitters, which would have helped in locating the pictures, unfortunately were not recorded. After about two-and-a-half years, Waldo journeyed back to New York, in January of 1809, with an English bride. Until the portrait of M'Dougle is found, whatever he learned in London can only be inferred from comparison of the few known portraits that he completed just before and after the trip. Luckily, he painted members of the Mumford family living near Lyme, Connecticut, at a time which can be pinpointed near the wedding date of the orphaned granddaughter, Mary Woodbridge, who married Henry Perkins in 1810. The surviving pictures of *Mrs. Henry Perkins* [Figure 122] and her younger sister,

Figure 122.
Mrs. Henry Perkins
(Mary Woodbridge)
Samuel L. Waldo
Oil on canvas, probably 1810
78.8 x 66.7 cm. (31 x 26¼ in.)
Private collection

Figure 123.
Lucretia Woodbridge
Samuel L. Waldo
Oil on canvas, probably 1810
76.2 x 63.5 cm. (30 x 25 in.)
Donald G. Mitchell
Not in exhibition

Samuel F. B. Morse

Lucretia Woodbridge [Figure 123], are evidence of considerable advance over Waldo's likeness of about 1803/4 of *James Gould* [Figure 124], one of his early Litchfield patrons. Most noticeably, he has a more sculptural sense of form and a new firmness in his drawing, which he may have acquired through his copies in chalk from the Academy's casts. From England, he had mentioned to Trumbull that he thought this exercise abroad would, in fact, "eventually be most to my advantage."[63]

Allston, who was to become a motivating force behind West's last students, returned to London in 1811 after an absence of about eight years. This time, he sailed from Boston with his wife and his young pupil, Samuel F. B. Morse (1791-1872). During his first period in London, Allston had shown unusual ability as well as a chameleon-like tendency to try a variety of subjects to which he adapted with considerable variation in style. He had developed an idiom of his own by the time of his second visit, and it was during this return that he rose to full

Figure 124.
James Gould
Samuel L. Waldo
Oil on canvas, circa 1803/4
73.6 x 61.6 cm. (29 x 24¼ in.)
Yale University Art Gallery,
New Haven, Gift of James Gould's
son, Edward S. Gould

stature as a history painter with such impressive works as *The Dead Man Restored* and *The Angel Releasing St. Peter from Prison*.

It was not an easy task for Allston to convince Morse's father, a rather stern Congregational minister, to send his son to London. Young Morse had done miniatures of his friends as a student at Yale and, when he graduated in 1810, he was certain that he should be a painter. But his parents had other ideas and wrote to him from Charlestown, Massachusetts, to "suspend" his mind on this issue until he could discuss it with them.[64] He soon conformed to their alternative—an apprenticeship under a bookseller—but, in the evenings, he built a fire in the room over the kitchen and, surrounded by his new lamp and painting equipment, indulged in his fondest dreams. Allston, working in nearby Boston, encouraged him, and Morse certainly knew Stuart as well. Aside from landscapes, Morse attempted a *Marius on the Ruins of Carthage* and *The Landing of the Pilgrims at*

Figure 125.
Self-Portrait
Samuel F. B. Morse
Oil on canvas, circa 1813
76.2 x 63.5 cm. (30 x 25 in.)
Addison Gallery of American Art,
Phillips Academy, Andover,
Massachusetts, Gift of
Mrs. Lelia Morse Rummel

Figure 126.
Self-Portrait
Samuel F. B. Morse
Watercolor on ivory, circa 1809
8.3 x 6.7 cm. (3¼ x 2⅝ in.)
National Academy of Design,
New York
Not in exhibition

Plymouth (both unlocated); but it was a landscape that caught Allston's eye and prompted him to approach the enterprising artist's father.[65]

Morse was in London for about six months, under the tutelage of Allston and, more distantly, West, when sixteen-year-old Charles Robert Leslie (1794-1859) arrived on the same quest from Philadelphia. The two students, close together in age with Morse three years older, found a common bond almost immediately in their mutual struggle, which was made stronger by a shared homesickness. They agreed to take rooms together, in December of 1811, in Great Titchfield Street, and, as Leslie recounted, "for some time we painted in one room, he at one window and I at the other.... Our Mentors were Allston and King."[66] In fact, these Americans, along with some English friends, formed a small coterie around the more experienced Allston. In one of his few letters after his departure, King gave poignant expression to the warmth of this friendship: *I have not been here sufficiently long to forget the delightful time when we could meet in the evening with novels, coffee, and* music by Morse, *with the conversation of that dear fellow Allston. The reflection that it will not again take place, comes across my mind accompanied with the same painful sensation as the thought that I must die.*[67]

At the Royal Academy, Leslie and Morse spent their evenings working from the casts. On the merit of a chalk sketch of the Laocoön, Morse was admitted for a year, in 1811, by the keeper of the Academy, Henry Fuseli, but he was never formally enrolled.[68] In contrast, Leslie was fully registered as a student— that is, he won the further approval of the Academy's Council—but not until March of 1813. Morse, apparently like some of the other American students, may have decided that he no longer profited from what the Academy had to offer. Fuseli was officially, as keeper, the supervisor of the Antique Academy, but, instead of criticizing drawings in progress, he was notorious for retiring behind a book until the end of the session. Nevertheless, the students appreciated his eccentric genius, and Leslie, years later, even praised him for the wisdom of his neglect.[69] Aside from the plaster replicas, the roommates drew from the Townley marbles in the British Museum, and later, in 1815, from the Elgin marbles, temporarily sheltered in the garden of Burlington House. For variation, during the summer, they painted in the nearby fields "before breakfast, and often before sunrise, to study the morning effect on the landscape."[70]

In a letter of January 30, 1812, to his parents, who were his financial support, Morse wrote that he had completed two landscapes and three portraits: "one of myself, one a copy from Mr. West's copy from Vandyke, and the other a portrait of Mr. Leslie, who is also taking mine." The likenesses that the students painted of each other, showing Morse, portrayed with a sense of humor, in a Scottish tartan, and Leslie in a Spanish cavalier's dress, are missing; but Morse's *Self-Portrait*, mentioned in the letter, might well be the small side-view on millboard which has recently come to light.[71] Apparently, it is the basis for a life-size copy [Figure 125] that Morse always said he had painted in London. Produced evidently with the aid of two mirrors, the original profile, in either version, is unquestionably an improvement over his earlier miniature *Self-Portrait* on ivory from about 1809 [Figure 126]. The ear, for instance, is not only better drawn

Charles Robert Leslie

Figure 127.
Self-Portrait
Charles Robert Leslie
Oil on canvas, 1814
75.9 x 52.9 cm. (29⅞ x 24¾ in.)
National Portrait Gallery, London

but now rather carefully modeled, although, admittedly, the treatment of the arm is still awkward. Leslie employed the same pose, almost exactly, in his profile *Self-Portrait* [Figure 127] of 1814, but his likeness is more technically advanced.

Like so many before him, Morse was captivated by the idealistic content of West's pictures as well as the sheer number and size of his works. Especially unforgettable was West's huge *Christ Healing the Sick* [Figure 5], which had to be copied for its intended owner, the Pennsylvania Hospital, because the first version was bought by the British Institution. Finding the master at work on the replica, Morse thought the sight of it worth the whole voyage to England, but Allston, with equal zeal, told Morse afterwards that West's *Christ Rejected by the Jews* [Figure 6], still in a preliminary stage, would be even better. Since the *Death of General Wolfe*, West had not won as much public approval as he did now. When *Christ Rejected*, a crowd scene with narrative appeal in the contrasting emotional reactions, was exhibited in a rented hall in June of 1814, nearly everyone went to see it. West's forte was generally accepted to be composition, while his faults were harsh outlines and inferior coloring; but sensitive disciples, such as young Morse, felt the acute injustice of this. His outlines, Morse concluded, had become softer, and his coloring was altogether admirable, better than that of any living artist. Often at this point in a defense of West, his devotees would curiously jump to a description of the master's fine personal character, as if this were indistinguishable from an assessment of his artistic ability. Indeed, in this period of fashionable moralizing, it was sometimes difficult to separate the two. Morse's account of West's work, seen during this studio visit, takes precisely this line: "He has just completed a picture . . . which . . . has never been excelled. In his private character he is unimpeachable. He is a man of tender feelings, but of a mind so noble that it soars above the slanders of his enemies."[72]

Morse's inclination to be a history painter had been evident even in America, but it was not until he was in London that he concentrated upon this end. He was encouraged particularly by West, who advised him "to paint *large* as much as possible."[73] The master provided invaluable help while Morse was laboring over his most ambitious work to date, the enormous *Dying Hercules* [Figure 128; color, page 130] intended for exhibition at the Royal Academy. Following Allston's lead in his *Dead Man Restored*, Morse first modeled in clay the figure he was to paint. Later, because it was so successful, he had the clay sculpture cast in plaster of Paris. The upward gesture of Hercules, straining against the poisoned cloth, is similar in pose to that of the revitalized man in Allston's *Dead Man Restored*, and yet appears to be more dependent upon a cast of the famous statue in Rome of the Laocoön (Vatican Museum). As in the Laocoön, the tensed muscles are exaggerated, even more so in Morse's painting than in the preliminary sculpture. The somber tones in the canvas version are certainly linked to Allston's palette, but the flesh colors are overworked. This had been one of Allston's criticisms of Morse's work in 1812—that the flesh was too muddy, as if molded from brick-dust and clay.[74] But both renditions of Morse's Hercules were considered outstanding. The plaster model won first prize, a gold medal, in a competition held by the Society of Arts, while the colossal painting was praised for its "very high merit" in a review of the Royal Academy's exhibition in the *London Globe*.[75]

Allston's criticisms were followed by constructive advice and reassurances that recall the methods of Benjamin West. His visits to Morse's studio were so frequent that he eventually became the artistic supervisor, not just of his original pupil, but of Morse's roommate, Leslie, as well. In this way, Allston filled a position reminiscent of Stuart in an earlier generation. It was a role sanctioned by West, who felt strongly, as he metaphorically stated, that "in a great family it remains with the parent at all times to counsel those, over whose education others are appointed."[76] But Morse insisted upon making a distinction between his teachers. "I am a pupil of Allston," he wrote in an early letter home, "and not

Figure 128.
Dying Hercules
Samuel F. B. Morse
Oil on canvas, 1812–13
244.4 x 198.7 cm. (96¼ x 78¼ in.)
Yale University Art Gallery,
New Haven, Gift of the Artist

Mr. West. They will not long ask who Mr. Allston is. . . . He claims me as his pupil, and told me . . . in a jocose manner, that he should have a battle with Mr. West unless he gave up all pretension to me."[77] Allston apparently liked having protégés. Leslie wrote to Morse, when Morse was in Bristol with Allston in 1814, that he was proud of being considered Allston's student: "Tell him, if he thinks it worth while to mention me at all . . . I shall consider it a great honor to be called his student."[78]

Leslie was thought to be a prodigy, and his first two years in London were partially financed by a group of Philadelphians, chiefly businessmen, so that he could become, in the later words of a contemporary art critic, "a finished miracle."[79] Like Sully, he was actually born in England, but his father was a Philadelphia watchmaker who returned to America in 1799 when Leslie was five

164

Figure 129.
The Personification of Murder
(photographed before painting was partially destroyed by fire)
Charles Robert Leslie
Oil on canvas, 1813
90.2 x 69.9 cm. (35½ x 27½ in.)
James R. Herbert Boone
Not in exhibition

years old. The windows of print shops, and his boyhood apprenticeship to a bookseller and publisher were evidently his first exposures to theatrical illustration which would become so important to him. The earliest of his drawings that attracted notice were of popular actors. Despite his young age and lack of experience, he even entered five such theatrical watercolor drawings in the annual exhibition of 1811 at the Pennsylvania Academy of the Fine Arts. The governing board of the school, modeled after the Royal Academy in England, decided that the sketches gave "promise of great celebrity" and granted him permission to enter as a student. Then, hearing of his intentions, which were evidently to study abroad, the Academy subscribed one-hundred dollars to assist in his career in London.[80] Sully, who was now established in Philadelphia, kindly gave him some lessons in oil painting and probably encouraged him to study in England.

Leslie's relationship with the Pennsylvania Academy seems always to have been a special one. He continued to exhibit there while he was still in London, and the Academy accorded him the unusual honor of what amounted to a one-man retrospective exhibition in 1816, when his earliest watercolor copies of prints were sentimentally touted as the signs of native genius.

At the Royal Academy, Leslie was awarded two silver medals for drawings (unlocated): one was done in Fuseli's antique class in 1814, from a cast of the Laocoön, and the other, a year later, was of a figure set in the life class by John Flaxman, the professor of sculpture. Probably under Fuseli's influence, Leslie found subjects of horror especially appealing at first. Instead of a classical or religious theme, he chose an allusion to *The Personification of Murder* [Figure 129] in *Macbeth* for his rather original contribution to the 1813 Royal Academy exhibition, and followed suit, in subsequent years, with *The Witch of Endor Raising the Ghost of Samuel Before Saul* (unlocated) in 1814, and *The Murder of Rutland by Lord Clifford* [Figure 130; color, page 131] in 1816.

Leslie's *Personification of Murder* (exhibited, as was the custom, with the passage it illustrated) was based on a clay maquette in the manner of Morse's *Hercules*, but the end result still had the caricatured quality of Leslie's Philadelphia drawings of actors. The staging of the dark, foreground cave from which Murder steals forth into the brilliant background moonlight, bent on one of his infamous missions, shows a keen sense of drama which was characteristic of Leslie. Both the *Murder* and his somewhat earlier *Timon of Athens* [Figure 131], again from Shakespeare and of approximately the same small size, were affected, in their anatomical drawing, by Leslie's innumerable studies from antique casts, and are almost monochromatic when compared to his later and larger *Murder of Rutland* from Shakespeare's *Henry VI*. One is acutely aware, here, of Leslie's growing sensitivity to the color and texture of paint. Young Rutland's sash, for instance, is a shimmering combination of maroon, peacock blue, and pale rose, while Clifford's armor gleams in the light at the fateful moment when he grabs the boy's angelic locks in one ironclad hand and raises his rapier in the other. The close-up, melodramatic treatment of the subject recalls the Shakespeare Gallery pictures of an earlier generation, most especially the work of James

Figure 130.
The Murder of Rutland by Lord Clifford
Charles Robert Leslie
Oil on canvas, 1815
245.8 x 202 cm. (96¾ x 79½ in.)
The Pennsylvania Academy of the Fine Arts, Philadelphia

Northcote. Although Leslie was evidently refining his aesthetic sensibility at this stage, he had not yet found his own particular métier.

Leslie apparently knew the styles of the principal English artists from the engravings after their works that he had seen in Philadelphia,[81] but it was not until he was actually in London that he experienced what he called a "dawning of taste." By this he meant, as expressed in a letter of 1812, that he now understood the merits of certain Old Masters, such as Titian and Veronese, that, for the sake of social acceptance, he had once only pretended to admire. Benjamin West was likewise a revelation: "the greatest painter that has appeared Since the memorable days of Michael Angelo and Raphael . . . I believe he has fewer faults than any painter that ever lived." Furthermore, "his drawing is Scientifically

167

Figure 131.
Timon of Athens
Charles Robert Leslie
Oil on canvas, 1812
91.4 x 71.1 cm. (36 x 28 in.)
The Athenaeum of Philadelphia,
Gift of William R. Talbot, Jr.,
in Memory of Frances K. Talbot

correct without reminding you of the dissecting room (as Fuseli & many others do)," and his coloring had improved so much, Leslie thought, that it was even "occasionally exquisite." He was almost equally impressed that West had "left no walk [subject] untried; I had no idea till I saw his gallery of the versatility of his genius."[82]

The young Philadelphian copied a number of West's paintings, including *King Alexander and the Stag Hunt* (1814; The Athenaeum of Philadelphia) in which West's rather dark outlines and propensity for highlighting is retained, and he was employed by West at least once as an assistant. In the reported instance, Leslie dead-colored a panel on which West was to paint a full-length *Self-Portrait*

168

(unlocated) to be presented to the Pennsylvania Hospital.[83] According to Leslie, West "spent a great deal of . . . time, in directing my studies."[84] He gave his student basic information on such problems as shading, the distribution of colors for a harmonious effect, and composition; and he was especially helpful while Leslie was working on his *Witch of Endor Raising the Ghost of Samuel Before Saul* (1814; unlocated), often visiting Leslie's painting room in order to give further advice. West took such a personal interest in the picture that, when it was sent to the British Institution for exhibition and refused because it was unvarnished, he suggested that Leslie varnish it and leave it in the Newman Street studio. Before long, the American patriarch sold it, with Leslie's consent, for one-hundred and five guineas to Sir John Leicester, one of the directors of the British Institution. Leslie, with great pleasure, then borrowed it back to enter in the Royal Academy exhibition of 1814.

The earliest known portraits in oil by Leslie are those executed in England, and include the 1812 likeness of *Nathaniel West* [Figure 132], a merchant from Salem, Massachusetts, so known for his frugality that he probably chose Leslie because the young student said that he would accept whatever payment was considered suitable.[85] By 1812, Leslie was a highly capable draftsman with an interest in clever illusion, such as in the three-dimensional letter that Nathaniel West holds or the highlighted hand which projects from Leslie's 1814 *Self-Portrait*. The *Nathaniel West* is rather broadly painted, with a special concern for the way in which flesh is illuminated by an all-pervading soft light. It reminds one of some of Allston's almost contemporary portraits—*Samuel Taylor Coleridge* (National Portrait Gallery, London) or *Benjamin West* [Figure 133]—where the head is constructed more in terms of light than shade. Allston, incidentally (whose tutoring consisted largely of instruction on color), thought that the portrait of Nathaniel West was "by far the best thing" that Leslie had done.[86]

Later, in about 1816, when Leslie finally ventured to paint a head of *Washington Allston* [Figure 134], the result was a more flashy demonstration of talent. Deliberately left in a sketchy state, it has the calculated effect of the same kind of effortless spontaneity for which Thomas Lawrence was known. The highlights in the eyes, the sheen on the curls, and the twist to the pose give it a kind of sparkling immediacy which is made more ingenious by contrast with the richly impasted collar and cravat, where the crudity of the medium is emphasized. Perhaps inspired by his admiration for the handsome and genteel Allston, Leslie produced a likeness which is rarely matched by his other portraits.

By 1816, Leslie's reputation as a portraitist was sufficiently established for him to be asked to paint the current American Ambassador to the Court of St. James's, *John Quincy Adams*, and his wife, *Louisa Johnson Adams* [Figures 135, 136]. Possibly because Adams had less time to sit, Leslie concentrated on the much more carefully modeled and intricately costumed likeness of Mrs. Adams. The suggestion of wistful reverie, the sunset background, and the low viewpoint are akin to Lawrence's romantic portraits, while the more summarily finished portrayal of Adams, the austere and independent intellectual, appears related to

Figure 132.
Nathaniel West
Charles Robert Leslie
Oil on canvas, 1812
76.2 x 63.5 cm. (30 x 25 in.)
Salem Marine Society, Massachusetts

Figure 133.
Benjamin West
Washington Allston
Oil on canvas, 1814
76.2 x 63.5 cm. (30 x 25 in.)
Library of the Boston Athenaeum

Figure 134.
Washington Allston
Charles Robert Leslie
Oil on canvas, circa 1816
66 x 45.7 cm. (26 x 18 in.)
National Academy of Design, New York,
Gift of Samuel F. B. Morse in 1865

Figure 135.
John Quincy Adams
Charles Robert Leslie
Oil on canvas, 1816
107.9 x 83.2 cm. (42½ x 32¾ in.)
Diplomatic Reception Rooms,
Department of State
Not in exhibition

Henry Raeburn's roughly blocked-in likenesses. Leslie's style clearly derived from his English contemporaries and yet was not really dependent on any single one of them.

Unlike Leslie, when faced with indications of a bleak future in history painting, Morse announced, with the dramatic stubbornness of his more volatile nature: "If I cannot live a gentleman, I will starve a gentleman."[87] Although he completed a couple of portraits in London, Morse was adamantly opposed to any kind of career as a limner. The idea "of lowering my noble art to a trade, of painting for money, of degrading myself and the soul-enlarging art which I possess, to the narrow idea of merely getting money" was absolutely repugnant.

Figure 136.
Louisa Johnson Adams
Charles Robert Leslie
Oil on canvas, 1816
92.7 x 73.6 cm. (36½ x 29 in.)
Diplomatic Reception Rooms,
Department of State

He undertook his profession as a history painter with a kind of missionary zeal which developed into a belligerent attitude, during the War of 1812, towards any English opposition. Extra-sensitive to the slightest inference of American inferiority, artistic or otherwise, his outlook in London was much more combative than that of his associates. "I should like to be the greatest painter," he wrote heatedly, "*purely out of revenge.*"[88]

When a gold medal and fifty guineas were offered by the Royal Academy in 1814 for the best picture of *The Judgement of Jupiter in the Case of Apollo, Marpessa, and Idas*, Morse was only too eager to enter the competition. His early sketches (Yale University Art Gallery) for the piece, most especially the *Head*

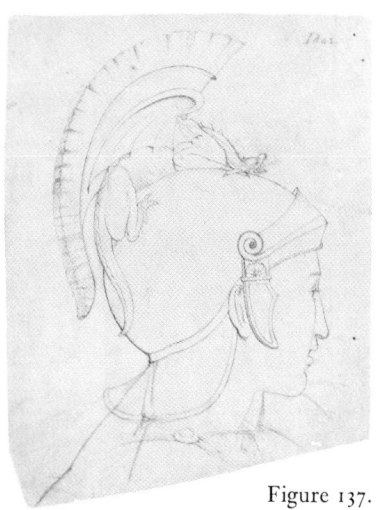

Figure 137.
Head of Idas
Samuel F. B. Morse
Graphite, 1814
17.2 x 13.2 cm. (6¾ x 5⁷⁄₁₆ in.)
Yale University Art Gallery,
New Haven

Figure 138.
Ulysses Giving Wine to Polyphemus
? Parker after John Flaxman
Engraving in Flaxman's
Illustrations to Homer, 1805
Library of Congress,
Washington, D.C.
Not in exhibition

of Idas [Figure 137], resemble John Flaxman's unshaded line-drawings from classical subjects, which were much admired and had appeared in book form [Figure 138]. Flaxman, by the way, was a near neighbor, at Number 7 Buckingham Place, Fitzroy Square, to Morse and Leslie who had moved into Mrs. Bridgen's boardinghouse at Number 8 in 1812.

Even some of Allston's drawings, perhaps especially after he transferred to Mrs. Bridgen's establishment when his wife died in 1815, reveal that he, too, could not escape the attraction of Flaxman's pure and elegant outlines. Allston's sketch of *Prometheus Bound* [Figure 139] and his tracings [Figure 140] from figures in his own painting of *Jacob's Dream* are the most obvious cases of influence.

Morse's *Judgement of Jupiter* [Figure 141], in which Jupiter acts as arbiter in a dispute over the woman Marpessa between Apollo and the mortal Idas, is actually a rather awkward pastiche of classical sources. The Apollo, for instance, is inspired by the famous fourth-century B.C. statue of the Apollo Belvedere, while the Marpessa appears to be ultimately derived from classical Nike figures; together the poses are very poorly related. Although the painting is now considered inferior to the *Dying Hercules*, West regarded it as exceptionally fine. He was certain that Morse would win the prize if he could meet the requirement of being present to receive it at the close of the competition in December of

Figure 139.
Prometheus Bound
Washington Allston
Ink on paper, circa 1812
10.8 x 13.4 cm. (5½ x 4¼ in.)
British Museum, London
Not in exhibition

Figure 140.
Two Groups of Angels from "Jacob's Dream"
Washington Allston
Brown ink on tracing paper, circa 1817
45.4 x 60 cm. (17⅞ x 23⅝ in.)
Fogg Art Museum, Harvard University, Cambridge, Massachusetts, The Washington Allston Trust Fund
Not in exhibition

Figure 141.
Judgement of Jupiter
Samuel F. B. Morse
Oil on canvas, 1814
126 x 103 cm. (49⅝ x 39½ in.)
Yale University Art Gallery, New Haven,
Gift of Russell Colgate, B.A., 1896
Not in exhibition

Figure 142.
Dorothea
Samuel F. B. Morse
Etching, 1814
12.7 x 8.2 cm. (5 x 3¼ in.)
The British Museum, London
Not in exhibition

1815. But that was not to be—Morse, at his parents' urging, had to return to Boston in August.

Before leaving, he did try a few subjects which were not in the grand historical style, but, otherwise, he was relentless in his determination to pursue only the highest form of art. His *Dorothea* (unlocated), from *Don Quixote*, was exhibited at the Royal Academy in 1814. Fortunately, with his tendency to experiment, Morse scratched out a small and somewhat crude etching from it, which still survives [Figure 142], and shows that this, too, is basically a classical quotation. The position of the arms is undoubtedly borrowed, in reverse, from the Royal Academy's cast of the well-known Capitoline Aphrodite.

Leslie had long been interested in contemporary literary illustration, but his complete conversion to this genre did not take place until after Morse's de-

Figure 143.
The Blind Fiddler
David Wilkie
Oil on canvas, 1806
57.8 x 79.4 cm. (22¾ x 31¼ in.)
The Trustees of The Tate Gallery, London
Not in exhibition

parture. He had pondered this course as early as 1813, when he decided that "pictures from modern poets do not take" and, to ensure success, a subject had to be either scriptural or classical.[89] Leslie was well aware of the chief contributors of contemporary illustration to the London exhibitions, among them Richard Westall and F. P. Stephanoff, but he still hesitated, and sent two scenes from Sir Walter Scott's popular poems to the 1813 exhibition at the Pennsylvania Academy, instead of to the Royal Academy. Unlike Morse, who was willing to swim upstream, Leslie tested the eddies to find an undercurrent. His early biographer, Tom Taylor, was mistaken in thinking that Leslie "dared to deviate" from the vogue for classical subjects.[90] Leslie was much more attuned to the public's taste in buying than Morse, whose work, though theoretically a challenge to the Italian Renaissance masters and respected by fellow-artists, held little appeal for the purchasing public which, towards the end of the eighteenth century, had become increasingly middle-class and less erudite. As Taylor noted (1860), many of Leslie's pictures "found a home among the mills of Lancashire and the smoking forges and grimy workshops of Birmingham,"[91] where they were appreciated as a civilized backdrop for the new manufacturing elite.

A number of factors, in concert, acted as a catalyst in Leslie's career decision. The rise in reputation of the English genre painter David Wilkie had been nothing less than meteoric ever since he first exhibited *The Blind Fiddler* [Figure

143] at the Royal Academy in 1807. By 1815, the newspaper reviews of the Royal Academy exhibitions tended to focus on two artists, West for history and Wilkie for narrative scenes from contemporary life.[92] Even West, as early as 1807, regarded Wilkie as superior to the Flemish Old Master, David Teniers, because Wilkie's facial expressions, he thought, were more emotionally convincing.[93] When Leslie traveled to Paris in 1817 with Allston and the English landscape and genre painter, William Collins, they were impressed by the fact that Collins's friend, Wilkie, was perhaps the most popular English artist in France.[94] More importantly, Leslie was undoubtedly affected by the recent exhibitions on Hogarth (1814) and Dutch and Flemish painting (1815), which included Teniers, Adriaen van Ostade, and Jan Steen, at the British Institution. Probably with the richness of color and characterization of this last show in mind, he varied his itinerary abroad to include a short excursion, on his return, through the Netherlands with Gilbert Stuart Newton, an American artist whom he had met in Paris.

Figure 144.
Sir Roger de Coverley Going to Church
Charles Robert Leslie
Oil on canvas, 1819
95.2 x 132.1 cm. (37½ x 52 in.)
Mrs. John F. Booth
Not in exhibition

Thus Leslie had a precedent and a stimulus for painting genre; and this was a small step away from literary illustration, not in the sense of the large Shakespeare Gallery pictures, but in the more salable "cabinet size." Both Wilkie and Collins had tried it, as well as Allston, who exhibited *Donna Mencia in the Robbers' Cavern* (Museum of Fine Arts, Boston), from *Gil Blas*, at the Royal Academy in 1815. Finally, Allston's friend, Washington Irving, helped to determine Leslie's future by engaging him with Allston, in 1817, to illustrate two of Irving's comical works, *History of New York* by "Knickerbocker" and *The Sketch Book*.

Leslie's first literary illustration to draw significant attention was his *Sir Roger de Coverley Going to Church* [Figure 144], which was entered at the Royal Academy in 1819 and later engraved. Painted for a friend, tobacco importer James Dunlop, the subject is taken from a well-known serial in an early eighteenth-century periodical called *The Spectator*. In this episode, Mr. Spectator, the narrator and a keen observer of manners, is shown with Sir Roger de Coverley, representative of country gentry. The picture was so successful, when shown, that the Marquis of Lansdowne commissioned a replica (Earl of Shelburne, Bowood), and Leslie started a new career with pictures of this sort as a specialty. Some of them are gently humorous or sentimental, and others are informative about the customs and costumes of the period portrayed, dutifully researched as would befit the student of *The Death of General Wolfe*. All of them are attractively composed with a decorative elegance typical of Leslie.

At last, in a most revealing letter of August 30, 1821, Leslie felt compelled to explain his chosen path to his long-time mentor and early friend. To Washington Allston, who had left England for the last time three years earlier, Leslie wrote: *You naturally wish to rouse me to do something in the style of art you are fondest of. But I believe I must for the present be content with an humble sphere. My inclinations lead me to subjects of familiar life and manners and what I have done in that way has been more successful than any thing else.* He added, "I have lately been studying the Dutch School a good deal and find my fondness for those admirable matter-of-fact painters increase in proportion to my acquaintance with them."[95] In this same year, Leslie was elected an Associate at the Royal Academy, and in 1826 an Academician, thus becoming the first of West's students to receive this honor. With the exception of a short interlude in America in 1833–34, Leslie, like Mather Brown before him, remained in England for the rest of his life.

Gilbert Stuart Newton

When he met Leslie in Paris, Gilbert Stuart Newton (1794-1835) was on his way to London from Italy. Born an English subject in Nova Scotia, he was taken, at age nine, by his mother to Charlestown, near Boston, where he later received some training as an artist under his uncle and namesake, Gilbert Stuart. Stylistically, in 1817, Newton was still highly impressionable. His Boston portraits are remarkably Stuartesque, while the scarce European ones are modified by a seductive confrontation with neoclassical standards. Newton and Leslie, the same age and with strong mutual interests, became immediate friends. Of the two, Newton was artistically less developed, but he had an admirable eye for color which Leslie seems to have appreciated.

Figure 145.
Thomas Palmer
Gilbert Stuart Newton
Oil on canvas, 1818/19
91.7 x 71.7 cm. (36⅛ x 28¼ in.)
Harvard University Portrait
Collection, Cambridge, Massachusetts,
Bequest of Thomas Palmer, 1820

The chronology of Newton's portraits has never been sufficiently established, but his likeness of *Thomas Palmer* [Figure 145], a wealthy Boston merchant in London, is certainly his earliest convincingly dated English work. Presented to the public at the Royal Academy in 1819, the painting is notable for its derivation from Allston's contemporary work. This is true particularly in the choice of flesh colors and the layered surface-glazing, as well as in the drawing and modeling of the hand which recalls Allston's best Michelangelesque manner. Although, on his arrival in London, Newton intended to paint portraits, he was soon persuaded to take the same path as Leslie but with Watteau as the chief source of inspiration for his figures. His literary illustration, much of which was engraved, gained him such respect that he was elected an Associate at the Royal Academy in 1828 and a full Academician in 1832.

Dunlap included Newton as a student of West in his list on the inside cover of one of his diary volumes, published after his lifetime, but not in his account of Newton in the *History of the Rise and Progress of the Arts of Design*, which was, of course, written to be published.[96] Given Newton's reputation since boyhood for affecting "to know so much," his dislike of regular study, and West's acknowledged state of physical decline by the year 1817, it does not seem likely that the relationship was anything but tenuous.[97] Newton, as we have seen, benefited from his short association with Allston before this charismatic figure departed for the States, but he appears to have been a pupil of West only in the most remote sense, through Leslie and Allston.

On the whole, these younger artists tended to experiment in various kinds of subject matter, so that we find Allston and Sully in landscape, King in still-life, and Morse, Leslie, and Newton in literary illustration. While the first generation were portrait painters, and the second chiefly history painters, this third group branched into new areas. They were not more imaginative or creative, but rather they were part of a general artistic movement in London, at the turn of the century, towards an increase in subject pictures other than history.[98]

Some of the American artists who traveled to London to learn the technical skills of their profession underwent a "dawning of taste," as Leslie called it, while they were there, which was an unexpected bonus, or perhaps a drawback. It meant the acquisition of a sense of quality which was not always understood at home. As the English chauvinist, Frances Trollope, was ready to observe during her visit to the United States in 1827-31, *From all the conversations on painting, which I listened to in America, I found that the finish of drapery was considered as the highest excellence, and next to this, the resemblance in a portrait; I do not remember ever to have heard the words* drawing *or* composition *used in any conversation on the subject.*[99] The "dawning of taste" involved an appreciation of the Old Masters in accordance with accepted English ideas of merit. Theoretically, the finest work was history painting, and, as one American cautioned Charles Willson Peale in 1767, "in this Part of the World few have a Taste for it."[100] In fact, Americans in general felt insecure before a history painting because they did not know how to judge it in the way that a portrait or landscape could be judged by comparison with nature. The realization that history painting would find even fewer buyers in America than in England came as the greatest blow to Samuel F.B. Morse and led to the termination of a painting career in deep disillusionment.

It was not just a problem of lack of American support, but of personal standards raised to unrealistic heights. "I have no wish to be remembered as a painter," Morse claimed in a letter of 1849, after he had invented the electric telegraph, "for I never was a painter. My ideal of that profession was, perhaps, too exalted—I may say is too exalted. I leave it to others more worthy to fill the niches of art."[101] Allston, too, suffered from a vision of greatness which he himself could not fulfill. While he dreamed of a synthesis of the best Old Masters, a few of his public-spirited Boston contemporaries set up a fund in 1820 to support him until his unfinished, colossal *Belshazzar's Feast* [Figure 146] could be completed, but their expectations only added to a creeping paralysis of self-doubt that he felt as a pioneer.

Trumbull, a generation earlier, with his small reportage pictures to be engraved, was more pragmatic. In contrast to Morse and Allston, he turned his sights on pleasing primarily an American rather than European audience, and with paintings which supposedly had an immediate documentary importance. In the end, his scheme was relatively successful. Although the engravings after his heroic battle scenes from the Revolutionary War never attracted the wide sale that Trumbull had expected, it was on the basis of the quality of the originals that he was finally commissioned, in 1817, to paint four life-size episodes from the Revolutionary War for the rotunda of the United States Capitol. By then,

Figure 146.
Belshazzar's Feast
Washington Allston
Oil on canvas, 1817–43
366 x 488 cm. (144⅛ x 192⅛ in.)
The Detroit Institute of Arts,
Gift of the Allston Trust
Not in exhibition

183

Figure 147.
Court of Death
Rembrandt Peale
Oil on canvas, 1820
350.5 x 713.7 cm. (138 x 281 in.)
The Detroit Institute of Arts
Not in exhibition

however, his ability had gone into a noticeable decline.

Actually, the only form of history that was truly destined for success in America, as Trumbull realized in time to make an additional profit with his government canvases, was the traveling road show. Where there was no one dominant artistic center and where there was a tradition of itinerancy among artists, it was a very natural and logical development. The most financially rewarding of these traveling pictures, treated as spectacles, was usually the huge Biblical scene. Thus, West's students Henry Sargent, William Dunlap, and Rembrandt Peale, late in life, produced religious narratives to meet the public's interest, particularly during the 1820s and 1830s, in large, sentimental, scriptural pieces. Their master's great Biblical cycles therefore had a second flowering in America, in the sense that the use of the same, or similar, subjects by these artists was certainly no coincidence. Into this category fall Sargent's *Christ Entering Jerusalem* (circa 1817, unlocated), Rembrandt Peale's *Court of Death* (1820 [Figure 147]), and Dunlap's *Christ Rejected* (circa 1820), *The Bearing of the Cross* (1823), *Christ on Calvary* (1825), and *Death on a Pale Horse* (1825), (all unlocated). The *Christ Rejected* and *Death on a Pale Horse* were admitted imitations of West's work.

In his late *Self-Portrait* (1819 [Figure 148]), West appears as the alert, forceful, and active man that he thought he still was; but the more reverential view of him, as an enthroned authority (even a relic from the past) with a transcendent spiritual strength, in Washington Allston's 1814 portrait, is, one suspects, more in keeping with the way Benjamin West's last students saw him. His greatest contribution as a teacher was certainly his ability to inspire enthusiasm in others. Dunlap really believed, in 1834, that "his influence on the art he professed will never cease."[102]

On the day after Benjamin West's death in 1820, his old servant asked what

Figure 148.
Self-Portrait
Benjamin West
Oil on canvas, 1819
82.2 x 65.1 cm. (32⅜ x 25⅝ in.)
National Collection of Fine Arts,
Smithsonian Institution,
Transfer from U.S. Capitol

so many were thinking: "Where will they go now?"[103] American painters would continue to come to London, but without the assurance of West's welcome. England, too, would miss him. Before West's death, Thomas Lawrence wrote worriedly to his fellow-Academician Joseph Farington, "I am more and more convinc'd that his Loss would be the greatest that the Arts in this Country could at this period suffer."[104] As West's successor at the Royal Academy, Lawrence later praised his "astonishing ability in age," which, "combined with the sacred importance of his subjects, gave him celebrity at the close of his life, far greater than he had ever before enjoyed; and he became (almost to forgetfulness of deceased greatness) the one popular painter of this country."[105] No matter what his failings, West was always held in esteem, most of all, by his fellow-artists.

Notes

1. Washington Irving's notes on Allston, Duyckinck Collection, The New York Public Library; or microfilm N 9, fr. 709 and fr. 716, Archives of American Art, Washington, D. C.

2. Letters, C. R. Leslie to Richard H. Dana, August 22, 1843, and William Collins to R. H. Dana, Sept. 6, 1843, Dana Papers, 1841-43, Massachusetts Historical Society, Boston.

3. According to William H. Gerdts's recent catalogue, *"A Man of Genius": The Art of Washington Allston (1779-1843)* (Museum of Fine Arts and the Pennsylvania Academy of the Fine Arts [Boston: 1979], p. 30), Allston painted a portrait of *Matthias Spalding* in London in 1801. But Spalding's rather complete diary and expense account, covering the entire period in London (May 15, 1801-September 26, 1802) exists and does not mention any such portrait (typescript in the possession of Mrs. Cecil C. Swann, Biltmore, North Carolina). It was probably painted later, around 1808.

4. Dunlap, *History*, vol. 2, pt. 1, p. 156.

5. Letter, W. Allston to Charles Fraser, August 25, 1801, Dana Papers, 1796-1808, Massachusetts Historical Society, Boston.

6. Letter of June 15, 1841, in Jared B. Flagg, *The Life and Letters of Washington Allston* (New York: 1892), p. 312.

7. Washington Irving's notes on Allston, Duyckinck Collection, The New York Public Library.

8. Flagg, *Allston*, pp. 188-89.

9. Dunlap, *History*, vol. 2, pt. 1, p. 159; James Northcote, *The Life of Sir Joshua Reynolds*, vol. 2 (London: 1818), p. 219.

10. Letter, W. Allston to Charles Fraser, August 25, 1801, Dana Papers, 1796-1808, Massachusetts Historical Society, Boston; Dunlap, *History*, vol. 2, pt. 1, p. 160, and vol. 1, p. 176.

11. Dunlap, *History*, vol. 2, pt. 1, p. 159.

12. Letter, W. Allston to Charles Fraser, August 25, 1801, Dana Papers, 1796-1808, Massachusetts Historical Society, Boston.

13. Flagg, *Allston*, p. 100.

14. Harold Edward Dickson, "Selections from the Writings of John Neal (1793-1876)," *The Pennsylvania State College Bulletin*, 37, no. 6 (February 5, 1943): xxiv.

15. Elizabeth B. Johns, "Washington Allston's Theory of the Imagination" (Ph.D. diss., Emory University, 1974), p. 16.

16. Leslie, *Autobiographical Recollections*, p. 179; Flagg, *Allston*, p. 90.

17. "Mr. Allston's Exhibition of Paintings," *The Bristol Gazette and Public Advertiser*, August 4, 1814.

18. Dunlap, *History*, vol. 1, p. 79.

19. Flagg, *Allston*, p. 121; letter (copy), W. Allston to John Vanderlyn, August 17, 1815, misfiled in Dana Papers, 1796-1808, Massachusetts Historical Society, Boston.

20. Farington, *Diary*, vol. 7, p. 180.

21. Flagg, *Allston*, p. 120.

22. *Ibid.*, p. 190.

23. William H. Gerdts, "Allston's 'Belshazzar's Feast,'" *Art in America* 61, no. 2 (March-April, 1973): 63; and *North American Review* (October 1840): 520.

24. Washington Allston, *Lectures on Art and Poems (1850) and Monaldi (1841)*, ed. Nathalia Wright (Gainesville, Fla.: 1967), p. 109.

25. Letter, W. Allston to J. F. Cogdell, July 1, 1826, in Flagg, *Allston*, p. 211.

26. Cunningham, *Lives of British Painters*, p. 43; Dunlap, *History*, vol. 1, p. 94.

27. Galt, *Life of Benjamin West*, pt. 2, pp. 79, 88-89, and 97.

28. *Ibid.*, pt. 2, p. 144.

29. *Ibid.*, pt. 2, pp. 94-95.

30. Benjamin West, *A Discourse Delivered to the Students of the Royal Academy (Dec. 10, 1792) . . . to Which is Prefixed the Speech of the President to the Royal Academicians (March 24, 1792)* (London: 1793), pt. 1, p. vi, and pt. 2, p. 27.

31. *A Tribute of Respect to the Memory of Benjamin West, Esq. . . . Who Died 11th March 1820* (London: n.d.), p. 5, microfilm N52, Archives of American Art; Galt, *Life of Benjamin West*, pt. 2, p. 97.

32. Quoted in letter (copy), C. W. Peale to Rembrandt Peale, November 17, 1809, vol. 10, p. 106, Charles Willson Peale's Letter Book, American Philosophical Society, Philadelphia.

33. C. Edwards Lester, *The Artists of America: A Series of Biographical Sketches of American Artists* (New York: 1846), p. 206; Rembrandt Peale, "Reminiscences," *The Crayon* 1, no. 19 (May 9, 1855): 290.

34. Lester, *Artists of America*, p. 206.

35. Letter (transcribed), A. G. D. Tuthill to Col. Sylvester Dering, August 26, 1799, Dering Letter Books, Shelter Island, New York.

36. Alfred Frankenstein and Arthur K. D. Healy, *Two Journeyman Painters* (Middlebury, Vt.: 1950), p. 53; Dunlap, *History*, vol. 2, pt. 1, p. 149.

37. See Frankenstein and Healy, *Two Painters*, p. 55, for a discussion of these as his English work.

38. Compare it to his 1798 likeness of the *Rev. Dr. Samuel Buell* (Long Island Historical Society) and to his portrait, painted just after his trip abroad, of *Cynthia Brown* (Oysterponds Historical Society, Inc.).

39. Dunlap, *History*, vol. 2, pt. 1, p. 18, quotes Malbone's 1801 letter, without a precise date, to Charles Fraser.

40. Letter, W. Allston to Charles Fraser, August 25, 1801, Dana Papers, 1796-1808, Massachusetts Historical Society, Boston.

41. Flagg, *Allston*, p. 12.

42. Dunlap, *History*, vol. 2, pt. 1, p. 19; Flagg, *Allston*, p. 36.

43. Notation in the facsimile of his account book reproduced in Ruel Pardee Tolman, *The Life and Works of Edward Greene Malbone (1777-1807)* (New York: 1958), p. 117.

44. Galt, *Life of Benjamin West*, pt. 2, pp. 166 and 172.

45. See Andrew J. Cosentino, *The Paintings of Charles Bird King (1785-1862)*, National Collection of Fine Arts (Washington, D. C.: 1977), p. 16.

46. The figures of Calypso and her companions in the Corcoran version appear to be by one of West's students.

47. Farington, *Diary*, vol. 7, p. 180, observation made in 1813 by Farington and Sir George Beaumont.

48. Letter, C. R. Leslie to his sister, February 25, 1813, in his *Autobiographical Recollections*, p. 187.

49. Thomas Sully's Journal (typescript), p. 10, Manuscript Archive, The New York Public Library.

50. Dickson, *John Neal*, p. 54.

51. Dunlap, *History*, vol. 2, pt. 1, p. 119.

52. *Ibid.*, p. 120.

53. Thomas Sully's Hints for Pictures (typescript), p. 3, Manuscript Archive, The New York Public Library.

54. Dunlap, *History*, vol. 2, pt. 1, p. 124.

55. Letter, Thomas Sully to Edward Peticolas, November 11, 1816, Valentine Museum, Richmond, Va.

56. Edward Biddle and Mantle Fielding, *The Life and Works of Thomas Sully* (New York: 1970), p. 15.

57. Dunlap, *History*, vol. 2, pt. 1, p. 119.

58. Letter, Thomas Sully to Daniel Wadsworth, June 17, 1810, Connecticut State Library, Hartford.

59. Dunlap, *History*, vol. 2, pt. 1, p. 127.

60. Letter (copy), C. W. Peale to Rembrandt Peale, July 6, 1810, vol. 11, p. 32, C. W. Peale's Letter Book, American Philosophical Society, Philadelphia.

61. Thomas Sully's Journal (typescript), p. 19, Manuscript Archive, The New York Public Library.

62. Letter, S. L. Waldo to John Trumbull, September 30, 1806, microfilm D5, fr. 332-34, C. H. Hart Papers, Archives of American Art, Washington, D.C.

63. *Ibid.*

64. Morse, *Letters*, vol. 1, p. 22.

65. Letter, S. F. B. Morse to Richard H. Dana, February 12, 1844, Marvin Sadik, Washington, D.C.

66. Leslie, *Autobiographical Recollections*, pp. 20-21.

67. Morse, *Letters*, vol. 1, p. 61.

68. *Ibid.*, p. 55.

69. Leslie, *Autobiographical Recollections*, pp. 25-26.

70. Summer of 1814. Morse, *Letters*, vol. 1, p. 162.

71. *Ibid.*, pp. 62-63. While this catalogue was in press, Robert G. Stewart and Ellen Miles came across the smaller version (10⅝ x 8¾ inches), nearly identical except for slight differences in detail, such as in the jabot, which make it appear to be closer to life.

72. *Ibid.*, pp. 44, 63, and 68.

73. *Ibid.*, p. 103.

74. Repeated in Morse's letter of May 25, 1812, *Ibid.*, p. 75.

75. Dunlap, *History*, vol. 2, pt. 2, p. 311.

76. West, *Discourse*, pt. 2, p. 2.

77. Morse, *Letters*, vol. 1, p. 105.

78. *Ibid.*, p. 156.

79. Dickson, *John Neal*, p. 16.

80. Decision of May 20, 1811. Microfilm of Correspondence, Documents, Rough Minutes, etc. of the Pennsylvania Academy of the Fine Arts, P63, fr. 240, Archives of American Art, Washington, D.C.; Dunlap, *History*, vol. 2, pt. 1, p. 242.

81. Leslie, *Autobiographical Recollections*, p. 20.

82. Letter (unpublished section), C. R. Leslie to Miss Leslie, April 19, 1812, Thomas L. Twidell, Groombridge, Kent, England. Leslie does not specify here which Old Masters he did not understand, but he does so in his *Autobiographical Recollections*, p. 22. I am grateful to Richard Kenin for telling me of the existence of the Twidell papers.

83. Dunlap, *History*, vol. 1, p. 86.

84. *Ibid.*, vol. 2, pt. 1, p. 243.

85. Leslie, *Autobiographical Recollections*, p. 182. Leslie finally received six pounds for it.

86. *Ibid.*, p. 181.

87. Morse, *Letters*, vol. 1, p. 164.

88. *Ibid.*, p. 133.

89. Leslie, *Autobiographical Recollections*, p. 194.

90. *Ibid.*, p. 213.

91. *Ibid.*, p. xviii.

92. "Press Cuttings," vol. 4, f. 939, Library of the Victoria and Albert Museum, London.

93. Nicholas B. Wainwright, "Conversations with Benjamin West," *The Pennsylvania Magazine of History and Biography* 102, no. 1 (January 1978): 110.

94. Leslie, *Autobiographical Recollections*, p. 28.

95. Letter, C. R. Leslie to W. Allston, August 30, 1821, Houghton Library, Harvard University, Massachusetts.

96. Dunlap, *Diary*, vol. 2, p. 543n.

97. Dunlap, *History*, vol. 2, pt. 2, pp. 300-1, 303, and vol. 1, pp. 86-87. Newton, however, did enroll as an Academy student in 1820.

98. See Catherine Gordon, "The Illustration of Sir Walter Scott: Nineteenth Century Enthusiasm and Adaptation," *Journal of the Warburg and Courtauld Institutes*, vol. 34 (London: 1971), p. 297, where she documents a change in exhibited subject matter between 1800 and 1830.

99. Frances Trollope, *Domestic Manners of the Americans*, ed. Donald Smalley (New York: 1949), p. 268.

100. Sellers, *Charles Willson Peale*, p. 62.

101. Morse, *Letters*, vol. 2, p. 31.

102. Dunlap, *History*, vol. 1, p. 33.

103. Leslie, *Autobiographical Recollections*, p. 38.

104. Undated letter, vol. 1, f. 164, Lawrence Papers, Library of the Royal Academy, London.

105. John Thomas Smith, *Nollekens and His Times*, ed. Wilfred Whitten, vol. 2 (London: 1920), p. 313.

Bibliography

MANUSCRIPTS

General

London. Victoria and Albert Museum. "Press Cuttings from English Newspapers on Matters of Artistic Interest, 1686-1835." 4 vols.

London. Royal Academy of Arts. Register of "Students Admitted in the Royal Academy from 1769 to 1827."

Washington Allston

Boston. Massachusetts Historical Society. Dana Papers, 1796-1808, 1841-1843.

New York. The New York Public Library. Duyckinck Collection. Washington Irving's Notes on Allston.

Mather Brown

Boston. Massachusetts Historical Society. Mather Brown's Correspondence, Byles Papers (loose); Mather Brown's Correspondence (typescript copies); and Letter Book of Mary and Catherine Byles, May 1793-August 1808 (transcript).

Cambridge, Mass. Harvard University. Letter, Charles Bulfinch to his mother, September 17, 1786. Copy in the Fogg Art Museum.

Washington, D.C. Library of Congress. Letter Book of William Temple Franklin.

Thomas S. Duché

Austin, Tex. Church Historical Society. Letter, Thomas S. Duché to the Rt. Rev. William White, August 7, 1789.

Philadelphia. Historical Society of Pennsylvania. Diary of Samuel Shoemaker. Letter, Thomas S. Duché to Mrs. John Morgan, June 7, 1783.

Ralph Earl

Deerfield, Mass. Deerfield Academy. Letter, Ralph Earl to Joseph Trumbull, September 23, 1784.

Robert Fulton

Chicago. Chicago Historical Society. Letter, Robert Fulton to David Morris, May 21, 1793.

New York. New-York Historical Society. Robert Fulton's Papers.

Washington, D.C. Archives of American Art. Microfilm P63, *Archives of the Pennsylvania Academy of the Fine Arts.* Letter, Robert Fulton to George Clymer, April 12, 1810.

Charles Robert Leslie

Cambridge, Mass. Harvard University. Houghton Library. Letter, Charles Robert Leslie to Washington Allston, August 30, 1821.

Groombridge, Kent, England. Thomas L. Twidell. Letter, Charles Robert Leslie to Miss Leslie, April 19, 1812.

Washington, D. C. Archives of American Art. Microfilm P63, *Correspondence, Documents, Rough Minutes, Etc. of the Pennsylvania Academy of the Fine Arts.*

Samuel F. B. Morse

Washington, D. C. Marvin Sadik. Letter, Samuel F. B. Morse to Richard H. Dana, February 12, 1844.

Charles Willson Peale

Philadelphia. American Philosophical Society. Letter Books of Charles Willson Peale.

Henry Sargent

Boston. Massachusetts Historical Society. Sargent Murray Gilman Hough House Papers, 1744-1886.

Philadelphia. Historical Society of Pennsylvania. Gratz Collection. Letter, Henry Sargent to William Dunlap, May 5, 1833.

Salem, Mass. Essex Institute. Henry Sargent's Papers.

Thomas Sully

Hartford, Conn. Connecticut State Library. Letter, Thomas Sully to Daniel Wadsworth, June 17, 1810.

New York. The New York Public Library. Manuscript Archive. Thomas Sully's Hints for Pictures, Thomas Sully's Journal (copy).

Richmond, Va. Valentine Museum. Letter, Thomas Sully to Edward Peticolas, November 11, 1816.

John Trumbull

New Haven, Conn. Yale University. Sterling Library. John Trumbull's Correspondence.

Washington, D.C. Library of Congress. Letter, John Trumbull to Thomas Jefferson, May 7, 1788.

Abraham G. D. Tuthill

Shelter Island, N.Y. Shelter Island Historical Society. Letter Books of Col. Sylvester Dering.

Samuel Lovett Waldo

Washington, D.C. Archives of American Art. Microfilm D5, C. H. Hart Papers. Letter, Samuel Lovett Waldo to John Trumbull, September 30, 1806.

Benjamin West

London, England. National Portrait Gallery. File of Autograph Letters. Letter, Benjamin West to Thomas Phillips, July 28, 1802.

London, England. Royal Academy of Arts. Papers of Thomas Lawrence.

New York. The New York Public Library. Berg Collection. Diary of Frances Burney, diary of Joseph Farington (microfilm of the typescript copy in the British Museum).

Philadelphia. Historical Society of Pennsylvania. Dreer Collection. Benjamin West's Correspondence.

Washington, D.C. Archives of American Art. Microfilm D23, Robert Graham Collection. Benjamin West's Correspondence.

DISSERTATIONS

Bassham, Ben Lloyd. "The Anglo-Americans: American Painters in England and at Home, 1800-1820." Ph.D. dissertation, University of Wisconsin, 1972.

Bolton, Kenyon C., III. "The Drawings of Washington Allston (A Catalogue Raisonné)." Ph.D. dissertation, Harvard University, 1977.

Cosentino, Andrew J. "Charles Bird King, 1785-1862." Ph.D. dissertation, University of Delaware, 1976.

Evans, Dorinda. "Mather Brown (1761-1831): A Critical Study." Ph.D. dissertation, Courtauld Institute of Art, 1972.

Green, Eleanor Broome. "Charles Robert Leslie." M.A. thesis, The George Washington University, 1971.

Johns, Elizabeth B. "Washington Allston's Theory of the Imagination." Ph.D. dissertation, Emory University, 1974.

Meyer, Jerry Don. "The Religious Paintings of Benjamin West: A Study in Late Eighteenth and Early Nineteenth Century Moral Sentiment." Ph.D. dissertation, New York University, 1973.

SECONDARY SOURCES

Ackermann, Rudolf. *The Microcosm of London*. 3 vols. London: 1808-9.

Addison, Julia De Wolfe. "Henry Sargent: A Boston Painter." *Art in America and Elsewhere* 17 (1929): 279-84.

Alberts, Robert C. *Benjamin West: A Biography*. Boston: 1978.

Allston, Washington. *Lectures on Art and Poems (1850) and Monaldi (1841)*. Edited by Nathalia Wright. Gainesville, Fla.: 1967.

"Mr. Allston's Exhibition of Paintings." *The Bristol Gazette and Public Advertiser*, August 4, 1814.

"American Painters." *American Quarterly Review* 17 (1835): 143-77.

"Benjamin West, Esq., President of the Royal Academy." *La Belle Assemblée* IV (1808): 5-9, 52-54, 109-11, 149-51, 197-98; Supplement: 13-20.

Bennett, Dr. H. Selfe. "The Story of Two Old Prints." *Art in America* 6 (1918): 240-48; 1964 reprint of volume.

Biddle, Edward, and Fielding, Mantle. *The Life and Works of Thomas Sully*. Reprint ed. New York: 1970.

Carey, William Paulet. *Observations on the Probable Decline or Extinction of British Historical Painting*. London: 1825.

Christie, Mr. *Catalogue of the First Part of the Superb Collection of Prints and Drawings Formed by the Late Benjamin West, Esq. R. A. . . . Which Will Be Sold by Auction . . . June the 9th, 1820, and Successive Days*. London: 1820.

_____.*Catalogue of the Last Part of the Superb Collection of Drawings, Prints, and Books of Prints, Formed by the Late Benjamin West, Esq. P.R.A. . . . Which Will Be Sold by Auction . . . July the 1st, 1820, and Successive Days*. London: 1820.

_____.*A Catalogue of the Truly Capital Collection of Italian, French, Flemish and Dutch Pictures Which Were Selected . . . by Benjamin West, Esq. P.R.A. . . . Which . . . Will be Sold by Auction . . . June the 23rd, 1820, and Following Day*. London: 1820.

Colden, Cadwallader D. *The Life of Robert Fulton*. New York: 1817.

Cosentino, Andrew J. *The Paintings of Charles Bird King (1785-1862)*. National Collection of Fine Arts. Washington, D.C.: 1977.

Cunningham, Allan. *The Lives of the Most Eminent British Painters, Sculptors, and Architects*. London: 1830.

Dickson, Harold Edward. "Selections from the Writings of John Neal (1793-1876)." *The Pennsylvania State College Bulletin* 37 (1943).

Dillenberger, John. *Benjamin West: The Context of His Life's Work with Particular Attention to Paintings with Religious Subject Matter*. San Antonio, Tex.: 1977.

Dillon, Sir William H. *A Narrative of My Professional Adventures (1790-1839)*. Edited by Michael A. Lewis. Second vol. never completed. London: 1953.

Du Fresnoy, Charles Alphonse. *De Arte Graphica: The Art of Painting*. Translated by John Dryden. London: 1695.

Dunlap, William. *Diary of William Dunlap (1766-1839)*. 3 vols. New York: 1931.

_____.*A History of the Rise and Progress of the Arts of Design in the United States*. Reprint ed. 2 vols. bound as 3. New York: 1969.

Evans, Grose. *Benjamin West and the Taste of His Times*. Carbondale, Ill.: 1959.

Farington, Joseph. *The Farington Diary*. Edited by James Greig. 8 vols. London: 1923-8.

Flagg, Jared B. *The Life and Letters of Washington Allston*. New York: 1892.

Flexner, James Thomas. *America's Old Masters*. New York: 1967.

_____.*Steam Boats Come True: American Inventors in Action*. 2nd edition. Boston: 1978.

Frankenstein, Alfred, and Healy, Arthur K. D. *Two Journeyman Painters*. Middlebury, Vt.: 1950.

Fulton, Eleanore J. "Robert Fulton as an Artist." *Papers Read Before The Lancaster County Historical Society* 42 (1938): 49-96.

Galt, John. *The Life of Benjamin West*. Edited by Nathalia Wright. Reprint ed. Gainesville, Fla.: 1960.

Gegenheimer, Albert Frank. "Artist in Exile: The Story of Thomas Spence Duché." *The Pennsylvania Magazine of History and Biography* 79 (1955): 2-26.

Gerdts, William H. "Allston's 'Belshazzar's Feast.'" *Art in America* (March-April 1973): 59-66; (May-June 1973): 58-65.

_____, and Stebbins, Theodore E., Jr. *"A Man of Genius": The Art of Washington Allston (1779-1843)*. Museum of Fine Arts. Boston: 1979.

Goodrich, Laurence B. *Ralph Earl: Recorder for an Era*. New York: 1967.

Gordon, Catherine. "The Illustration of Sir Walter Scott: Nineteenth Century Enthusiasm and Adaptation." *Journal of the Warburg and Courtauld Institutes* 34 (1971): 297-317.

Graves, Algernon. *The British Institution, 1806-1867: A Complete Dictionary of Contributors and Their Work from the Foundation of the Institution*. Reprint ed. Bath, England: 1969.

_____. *The Society of Artists of Great Britain 1760-1791, The Free Society of Artists 1761-1783: A Complete Dictionary of Contributors and Their Work from the Foundation of the Societies to 1791*. Reprint ed. Bath: 1969.

_____. *Royal Academy of Arts: A Complete Dictionary of Contributors and Their Work from its Foundation in 1769 to 1904*. 8 vols. London: 1905.

Gwynn, Stephen. *Memorials of an Eighteenth Century Painter (James Northcote)*. London: 1898.

Hazlitt, William. *Criticism on Art*. 2d ser. London: 1844.

Henkels, Stan V. *Addenda to Sale of Autographs, Friday, June 8, 1917. . . .* Philadelphia: 1917.

Hunt, Leigh. *The Autobiography of Leigh Hunt, with Reminiscences of Friends and Contemporaries*. 2 vols. Reprint ed. New York: 1965.

Hutchison, Sidney C. *The History of the Royal Academy, 1768-1968*. London: 1968.

_____. "The Royal Academy Schools: 1768-1830." *The Walpole Society* 38 (1962): 123-91.

Jaffe, Irma B. *John Trumbull: Patriot-Artist of the American Revolution*. Boston: 1975.

Johns, Elizabeth. "Washington Allston's *Dead Man Revived*." *The Art Bulletin* (March 1979): 78-99.

Johns, Elizabeth, and Bolton, Kenyon C., III. *The Paintings of Washington Allston*. Lowe Art Museum. Miami: 1975.

Jones, Guernsey, ed. *Letters and Papers of John Singleton Copley and Henry Pelham, 1739-1776*. Reprint ed. New York: 1970.

Jordan, John W. "The Fellowship Fire Company of Philadelphia, Organized 1738." *The Pennsylvania Magazine of History and Biography* 27 (1903): 472-81.

Kraemer, Ruth S. *Drawings by Benjamin West and His Son Raphael Lamar West*. The Pierpont Morgan Library. New York: 1975.

La Roche, Sophie von. *Sophie in London, 1786*. Translated by Clare Williams. London: 1933.

"The Late Mather Brown, Esq." *Library of the Fine Arts* 1 (1831-1832): 453-56.

Leslie, Charles Robert. *Autobiographical Recollections by the Late Charles Robert Leslie, R.A.* Edited by Tom Taylor. London: 1860.

Leslie, Charles Robert, and Taylor, Tom. *Life and Times of Sir Joshua Reynolds*. 2 vols. London: 1865.

Lester, C. Edwards. *The Artists of America: A Series of Biographical Sketches of American Artists.* New York: 1846.

Mitchell, Charles. "Benjamin West's 'Death of Wolfe' and the Popular History Piece." *Journal of Warburg and Courtauld Institutes* 7 (1944): 20-33.

Morgan, John Hill. *Gilbert Stuart and His Pupils.* New York: 1939.

Morgan, John S. *Robert Fulton.* New York: 1977.

The Morning Herald, May 2, 1809.

Morse, Edward Lind. *Samuel F. B. Morse: His Letters and Journals.* 2 vols. Boston: 1914.

North American Review, October 1840.

Northcote, James. *The Life of Sir Joshua Reynolds.* 2 vols. London: 1818.

Peale, Rembrandt. "Reminiscences." *The Crayon* 1 (1855): 290-91.

Pleasants, J. Hall. "George William West: A Baltimore Student of Benjamin West." *Art in America* 37 (1949): 6-47.

Prown, Jules D. *John Singleton Copley.* 2 vols. Cambridge, Mass.: 1966.

The Queen's Gallery. *George III: Collector & Patron.* London: 1974-75.

Ralph, Benjamin. *The School of Raphael: Or the Student's Guide to Expression in Historical Painting.* London: 1759.

Reynolds, Graham. *Constable: The Natural Painter.* New York: 1965.

Richardson, E. P. *Gilbert Stuart: Portraitist of the Young Republic, 1755-1828.* National Gallery of Art. Washington, D.C.: 1967.

_____. *Washington Allston: A Study of the Romantic Artist in America.* New York: 1967.

Richardson, Jonathan. *An Essay on the Theory of Painting.* London: 1725.

Robins, George. *A Catalogue of a Few Finished Original Pictures . . . Works of the late Benjamin West, Esq. P.R.A. . . . Which Will Be Sold by Auction . . . the 20th and 22nd June, 1829.* London: 1829.

_____. *A Catalogue Raisonné of the . . . Historical Pictures, and Other Admired Compositions, the Works of . . . Benjamin West, Esq. . . . May 22d, 23d, and 25th, 1829.* London: 1829.

Rutledge, Anna Wells. *Artists in the Life of Charleston.* Philadelphia: 1949.

_____. *Cumulative Record of Exhibition Catalogues. The Pennsylvania Academy of the Fine Arts, 1807-1870; The Society of Artists, 1800-1814; The Artist's Fund Society, 1835-1845.* Philadelphia: 1955.

Sartain, John. *The Reminiscences of a Very Old Man, 1808-1897.* Reprint ed. New York: 1969.

Sawitzky, William. *Matthew Pratt: 1734-1805.* New York: 1942.

_____, and Susan. "Two Letters from Ralph Earl with Notes on His English Period." *Worcester Art Museum: Annual Report for the Year 1960* 8 (1961): 8-41.

Sellers, Charles Coleman. *Patience Wright: American Artist and Spy in George III's London.* Middletown, Conn.: 1976.

_____. *Charles Willson Peale.* New York: 1969.

_____. *Portraits and Miniatures by Charles Willson Peale.* Reprint ed. Philadelphia: 1968.

_____."Rembrandt Peale, 'Instigator.'" *The Pennsylvania Magazine of History and Biography* 79 (1955): 331-42.

Sherman, Frederic Fairchild. "James Earl: A Forgotten American Portrait Painter." *Art in America and Elsewhere* 23 (1935): 143-53.

Sizer, Theodore. *The Works of Colonel John Trumbull, Artist of the American Revolution*. New Haven: 1967.

_____, ed. *The Autobiography of Colonel John Trumbull, Patriot-Artist, 1756-1843*. New Haven: 1953.

Smith, John Thomas. *Nollekens and His Times*. Edited by Wilfred Whitten. 2 vols. London: 1920.

Spencer, Harold. *The American Earls: Ralph Earl, James Earl, R. E. W. Earl*. The William Benton Museum of Art. Storrs, Conn.: 1972.

Stewart, Robert G. *Henry Benbridge (1743-1812): American Portrait Painter*. National Portrait Gallery. Washington, D.C.: 1971.

Sutcliffe, Alice Crary. *Robert Fulton*. New York: 1930.

Swan, Mabel Munson. *The Athenaeum Gallery, 1827-1873*. Boston: 1940.

Tolman, Ruel Pardee. *The Life and Works of Edward Greene Malbone (1777-1807)*. New York: 1958.

A Tribute of Respect to the Memory of Benjamin West, Esq. . . . Who Died 11th March 1820. London, n.d. Microfilm N52. Archives of American Art, Washington, D.C.

Trollope, Frances. *Domestic Manners of the Americans*. Edited by Donald Smalley. New York: 1949.

Wainwright, Nicholas B. "Conversations with Benjamin West." *The Pennsylvania Magazine of History and Biography* 102 (1978): 109-14.

Wark, Robert R., ed. *Sir Joshua Reynolds: Discourses on Art*. San Marino, Calif., 1959.

West, Benjamin. *A Discourse Delivered to the Students of the Royal Academy, (Dec. 10, 1792) . . . to Which is Prefixed the Speech of the President to the Royal Academicians (March 24, 1792)*. London: 1793.

Whitley, William T. *Artists and Their Friends in England, 1700-1799*. 2 vols. New York: 1968.

_____. *Gilbert Stuart*. Cambridge, Mass.: 1932.

Williamson, Dr. [George Charles]. *John Downman, A.R.A*. London: 1907.

Wilmerding, John. *American Art*. New York: 1976.

Wind, Edgar. "Penny, West and the 'Death of Wolfe.'" *Journal of the Warburg and Courtauld Institutes* 10 (1947): 159-62.

Wortis, Helen. "A.G.T. [*sic*] Tuthill of Oyster Ponds." *Long Island Forum* 39 (1976): 218-22.

Index

Allston, Washington 11, 12, 132–41, 158–61, 163, 169, 180, 181, 183
  The Angel and Three Marys 139
  The Angel of Wrath 139
  The Angel Releasing St. Peter from Prison 139, 141, 159; Fig. 103
  Belshazzar's Feast 139, 183; Fig. 146
  Benjamin West 169; Fig. 133
  Christ Healing the Sick 139
  The Dead Man Restored to Life by Touching the Bones of the Prophet Elisha 137, 138, 139, 141, 159, 163; Fig. 102
  Donna Mencia in the Robbers' Cavern 180
  French Soldier Telling a Story 133
  Judas Iscariot 132
  Landscape 134; Fig. 100
  Peter Hearing the Cock Crow 132
  Prometheus Bound 174; Fig. 139
  A Rocky Coast with Banditti 132; Fig. 98
  Samuel Taylor Coleridge 169
  Saul and the Witch of Endor 139
  Self-Portrait 132; Fig. 99
  The Tippler 132
  Tragic Figure in Chains 132; Fig. 97
  Two Groups of Angels from "Jacob's Dream" 174; Fig. 140
  Uriel in the Sun 139

Barry, James 75
Beaumont, Sir George 139
Benbridge, Henry 33
  Pascal Paoli 32; Fig. 15
Boydell's Shakespeare Gallery 93
Brown, Mather 11, 12, 74–83, 93–101
  Annunciation of the Virgin 93
  The Duke of Norfolk Receiving from Henry VIII an Augmentation to His Coat-of-Arms in Consequence of the Victory of Flodden Field, 1513 97
  Duke of York 81; Fig. 56
  Finding of Moses 98; Fig. 72
  Frederick W. Geyer 77; Fig. 52
  Girl at a Harpsichord 75; Fig. 50
  John Adams 80
  Lord Howe on the Deck of the "Queen Charlotte" 97
  Moses Striking the Rock 101; Fig. 75
  Oil Sketch for The Battle of the Nile 99; Fig. 73
  Passion of Our Saviour in the Garden of Gethsemane 93; Fig. 67
  Portrait of a Gentleman 76, 78; Fig. 53
  Prince of Wales 81
  Thomas, Earl of Surrey, Son of John, 1st Duke of Norfolk, Defending His Allegiance to Richard III before Henry VII after the Battle of Bosworth Field, 1485 97; Fig. 70
  Thomas Jefferson 80; Fig. 55
  Thomas Paine 80
Burney, Fanny 19

College at Philadelphia 14
Collins, William 132, 179
Columbianum 46
Constable, John 21
Copley, John Singleton 34–37, 52, 60, 61, 62, 71, 73, 81, 89–90, 91
  Boy With a Squirrel 34; Fig. 18
  The Death of the Earl of Chatham 90; Fig. 65
  The Death of Major Peirson 89; Fig. 64
  Watson and the Shark 111
Correggio 24
  Madonna of St. Jerome 24
Cosway, Richard 146
Cotes, Francis 39

Dance, Nathaniel 58
Davy, Robert 117
Delanoy, Abraham 11, 28, 33, 40
  Archibald Laidlie, D.D. 33; Fig. 17
  Beekman family portraits 33
  Benjamin West 33; Fig. 16
  Venus and Cupid (copy after Benjamin West) 33
Downman, John 30
Duché, Thomas Spence 11, 12, 106–10
  Charity Presenting a Prostitute to Three Reclaimed Females at the Magdalen Hospital 107
  Esther Duché 106, 108; Fig. 83

Hope Delivering Two Orphan Girls to the Genius of the Asylum 107
Reverend Samuel Seabury 108; Fig. 85
Thomas Spence Duché and His Father Jacob 107; Fig. 84
Du Fresnoy, Charles Alphonse 14, 37
Dunlap, William 11, 12, 22, 28, 34, 60, 66, 71, 110, 111–12, 117, 184
The Artist Showing a Picture from "Hamlet" to His Parents 111; Fig. 87
The Bearing of the Cross 184
Choice of Hercules (after Benjamin West) 111
Christ on Calvary 184
Christ Rejected 184
Death on a Pale Horse 184
Ferrau Gazing with Horror upon the Ghost 111
George Washington 111; Fig. 88
Washington at Princeton 111
Watson and the Shark (after John Singleton Copley) 111

Earl, James 11, 110–11
Lady Caroline Beauclerk 111
Portrait of an Unknown Gentleman 111; Fig. 86
A Small Head 111
Two Boys 111
Earl, Ralph 11, 52, 60–66, 110
Ann Whiteside 64; Fig. 44
Colonel George Onslow, M.P. 61; Fig. 42
Joseph Trumbull 63; Fig. 43
Lady Williams and Child 62
Mary Ann Carpenter 61; Fig. 39
A Master in Chancery Entering the House of Lords 62
Mrs. John Johnston 61; Fig. 41
Reclining Hunter 64; Fig. 45
The Rev. and Mrs. Timothy Dwight 60
Roger Sherman 61; Fig. 40
William Carpenter 61

Flaxman, John 174
Ulysses Giving Wine to Polyphemus 174. See Parker
Free Society of Artists 33
Fulton, Robert 11, 12, 116–20
Charles, 3rd Earl Stanhope 117; Fig. 93
Elisha Raising the Widow's Son 119
Joseph Bringhurst 118; Fig. 94
Lady Jane Grey the Night Before Her Execution 119
Louis XVI in Prison Taking Leave of His Family 119
Mary Queen of Scots Under Confinement 119
Priscilla and Alladine, from Spenser's Faerie Queene 119
Fuseli, Henry 132, 136, 154, 161, 166

Gainsborough, Thomas 51, 53, 54, 65
Blue Boy 51; Fig. 31

Galt, John 14, 16, 22
George III 15, 18–19, 43, 48, 50, 88, 120

Halpin, John Edmund 113, 115
Hunt, Leigh 66

Incorporated Society of Artists 54

Jennings, Samuel 113
Johnston, John 113, 115
Judge David Sewall 115; Fig. 91

King, Charles Bird 11, 12, 146–51, 161
Boy Stealing Fruit from His Sister 147
Children and Bubble 147
Dr. David King 149; Fig. 113
Lear and Cordelia 147
Self-Portrait 149; Fig. 114
Still Life, Game 148; Fig. 112
Telemachus and Calypso (after Benjamin West) 148
Kingsbury, Henry 50
Major Peter Labilliere (after Joseph Wright) 50; Fig. 29

Lawrence, Thomas 21, 145, 185
Le Keux, John
West's Picture Gallery (after Cattermole) Fig. 46
Leslie, Charles Robert 11, 12, 22, 132, 137, 161–62, 163–70, 177–80
John Quincy Adams 169; Fig. 135
King Alexander and the Stag Hunt (after Benjamin West) 168
Louisa Johnson Adams 169; Fig. 136
The Murder of Rutland by Lord Clifford 166; Fig. 130
Nathaniel West 169; Fig. 132
The Personification of Murder 166; Fig. 129
Samuel F. B. Morse 161
Self-Portrait 162, 169; Fig. 127
Sir Roger de Coverley Going to Church 180; Fig. 144
Timon of Athens 166; Fig. 131
Washington Allston 169; Fig. 134
The Witch of Endor Raising the Ghost of Samuel Before Saul 166, 169
Lovett, William 113

Malbone, Edward G. 11, 12, 132, 144, 145–46
Colonel Thomas Pinckney, Jr. 146; Fig. 110
The Hours 146; Fig. 109
Washington Allston 145, 146; Fig. 107
Mengs, Anton Raphael 14
Morse, Samuel F. B. 11, 12, 158–64, 172–77, 182
Charles Robert Leslie 161
Dorothea 177; Fig. 142
Dying Hercules 163; Fig. 128
Head of Idas 174; Fig. 137
Judgement of Jupiter 174; Fig. 141
The Landing of the Pilgrims at Plymouth 159

Marius on the Ruins of Carthage 159
Self-Portrait (two likenesses) 161; Figs. 125, 126
Mortimer, John Hamilton 155
Bandit Taking Up His Post 155; Fig. 118

Newton, Gilbert Stuart 11, 12, 179, 180–82
Thomas Palmer 181; Fig. 145
Northcote, James 22

Orme, Daniel
Lord Howe on the Deck of the "Queen Charlotte" (after Mather Brown) Fig. 69

Parker, ?
Ulysses Giving Wine to Polyphemus (after John Flaxman) Fig. 138
Peale, Charles Willson 11, 12, 30, 33, 37–46, 86, 142, 155
George Washington 72
Girl with a Toy Horse 40; Fig. 22
Matthias and Thomas Bordley 40; Fig. 21
William Pitt 44; Fig. 25
Peale, Rembrandt 11, 12, 142–43, 150, 184
Court of Death 184; Fig. 147
George Washington 142
Rubens Peale with a Geranium 142; Fig. 105
Sir Joseph Banks 142; Fig. 104
The Pennsylvania Academy of the Fine Arts 166
Pratt, Matthew 11, 24–32, 33, 44
The American School 27–29; Cover, Fig. 13
Benjamin Franklin (after 1761 engraving, after Benjamin Wilson) 24
Benjamin West 26, 33; Fig. 11
Elizabeth Moore 24; Fig. 8
Elizabeth Shewell West 26; Fig. 12
A Fruit Piece 24
Jupiter and Europa (after Guido Reni) 24
Madonna of St. Jerome 24; Fig. 7
Self-Portrait 25; Fig. 9
Venus and Cupid (after Benjamin West) 24

Reni, Guido 24
Jupiter and Europa 24
Reynolds, Joshua 16, 19, 22, 34, 39, 44, 54, 63, 75, 78, 84–85, 136, 141
Richardson, Jonathan 14, 37
Robertson, Andrew 144
Benjamin West 145
Romney, George 53, 63
Rosa, Salvator 133
Royal Academy of Arts 18, 19, 20, 33, 34, 44, 46, 48, 74, 81, 93, 120, 166
Rubens, Peter Paul 52
Self-Portrait 52; Fig. 34

St. Martin's Lane Academy 44
Sargent, Henry 11, 113–15, 184
Captain Joseph McLellan, Sr. 115; Fig. 90
Christ Entering Jerusalem 184
Edwin and Angelina 113
Mr. Hanger 113
Sartain, John 68
Sharp, William 108
Shelley, Samuel 146
The Hours 146; Fig. 108
Shewell, Betsy. *See* Betsy Shewell West
Smith, The Reverend William 14
Society of Artists of Great Britain 16, 18
Stuart, Gilbert 11, 12, 21, 52–58, 66, 69, 73, 76–81, 144, 154
Dr. Benjamin Waterhouse 52; Fig. 32
Henrietta Elizabeth Frederica Vane 54; Fig. 37
James Ward 54; Fig. 36
John Trumbull (and John Trumbull) Fig. 49
Portrait of a Gentleman 52
Self-Portrait 52; Fig. 33
The Skater 55; Fig. 38
William Woollett 78; Fig. 54
Sully, Thomas 11, 12, 29, 146, 151–56
Charles Bird King 151
Joseph Dugan 156; Fig. 121
Fielding Lucas 155; Fig. 120
Pylades and Orestes (after Benjamin West) 151; Fig. 115
Self-Portrait 155; Fig. 119
Stoke Park, Sir Edward Coke's Column 154; Fig. 116
Telemachus and Calypso (after Benjamin West) 153
William B. Wood as "Charles de Moor" 155; Fig. 117

Trumbull, John 11, 12, 71–74, 83–93, 97, 100, 113, 114, 183–84
Battle of La Hogue (and Benjamin West) 86; Fig. 60
The Dancing Faun 83; Fig. 57
The Death of General Montgomery in the Attack on Quebec, December 31, 1775 89, 90; Fig. 63
The Death of General Warren at the Battle of Bunker's Hill, June 17, 1775 89; Fig. 62
The Death of General Wolfe (after Benjamin West) 86
The Deluge 101; Fig. 77
George Washington (half-length portrait, after Charles Willson Peale) 72
George Washington (full-length portrait) 72; Fig. 47
Infant Saviour with St. John the Baptist Dressing the Lamb with Flowers 100; Fig. 74
John Trumbull (and Gilbert Stuart) Fig. 49
Joseph Trumbull 72; Fig. 48
Jeremiah Wadsworth and His Son, Daniel 84; Fig. 58
Our Saviour with Little Children 100
Priam Returning with the Body of Hector 86, 87, 88; Fig. 61
Sir John Temple 85; Fig. 59
The Sortie Made by the Garrison of Gibraltar, November 27, 1781 92; Fig. 66

Tuthill, Abraham G. D.   11, 144–45
   Benjamin West   145; Fig. 106
   Nativity   145

Van Dyck, Sir Anthony   54

Waldo, Samuel L.   11, 12, 146, 156–58
   James Gould   158; Fig. 124
   Lucretia Woodbridge   158; Fig. 123
   Mr. M'Dougle   156, 157
   Mrs. Henry Perkins   157; Fig. 122
Ward, James
   Lady Jane Grey the Night Before Her Execution (after Robert Fulton)   Fig. 96
   Mary Queen of Scots Under Confinement (after Robert Fulton)   Fig. 95
West, Benjamin
   Agrippina Landing at Brundisium with the Ashes of Germanicus   17; Fig. 3
   Angelica and Medoro   15; Fig. 2
   Angel in the Sun   104, 139; Fig. 81
   Battle of Crécy   92
   Battle of La Hogue (and John Trumbull)   86; Fig. 60
   The Call of Isaiah   95; Fig. 68
   The Call of Jeremiah   95
   Cave of Despair   46; Fig. 27
   Charles Willson Peale   42; Fig. 23
   Choice of Hercules   111
   Christ Healing the Sick in the Temple (first version)   19, 139, 162
   Christ Healing the Sick in the Temple (second version)   19, 98, 151; Fig. 5
   Christ Rejected by the Jews   19, 68, 98, 135, 163; Fig. 6
   Cimon and Iphigenia   15
   The Cricketers   27; Fig. 14
   Cromwell Dissolving the Long Parliament   98; Fig. 71
   The Death of the Chevalier Bayard   46; Fig. 26
   The Death of General Wolfe   13, 20, 46, 80, 86, 89; Fig. 1
   The Death of General Wolfe (copy)   19, 163
   Death of Socrates   14
   Death on a Pale Horse   19, 68, 134; Fig. 101
   The Departure of Regulus   43, 87; Fig. 24
   Diana Mary Barker   26; Fig. 10
   Diomed and His Horses Stopped by the Lightning of Jupiter   104

   The Drummond Family   76; Fig. 51
   Elisha Raising the Shunammite's Son   37; Fig. 20
   Governor James Hamilton   30, 37; Fig. 19
   King Alexander and the Stag Hunt   168
   Last Supper   19, 88; Fig. 4
   Madonna of St. Jerome (after Correggio)   24
   Moses Striking the Rock   Fig. 76
   Omnia Vincit Amor   151
   Parting of Hector and Andromache   16
   Pylades and Orestes   151
   Raphael and Benjamin West, Sons of the Artist   Fig. 78
   Return of the Prodigal Son   16
   Robert Fulton   116; Fig. 92
   Self-Portrait   52, 169, 184; Figs. 35, 148
   Telemachus and Calypso   93, 148, 153; Fig. 111
   The Trial of Susannah   14
   Venus and Cupid   24, 33
   William Penn's Treaty with the Indians   46
West, Benjamin, Jr.   71, 103
West, Betsy Shewell   24, 71
West, George William   11, 112–13
   Figure Sketches   113; Fig. 89
West, Raphael Lamar   11, 71, 103–4, 111
   Brigand Lying Under a Tree   104; Fig. 80
   Cadmus Slaying the Dragon   103; Fig. 79
   Orlando Rescuing Oliver From the Lion and the Serpent   104
Wilkie, David   178–79
   The Blind Fiddler   178; Fig. 143
Williams, William   14
Wilson, Benjamin   24
   Benjamin Franklin   24
Wilson, William Charles   104
   Orlando Rescuing Oliver from the Lion and the Serpent (after Raphael Lamar West)   Fig. 82
Woollett, William   20
   The Death of General Wolfe (after Benjamin West)   20, 80
Wright, Joseph   11, 48–51
   John Coats Browne   51; Fig. 30
   Major Peter Labilliere   50
   Patience Wright   49
   Portrait of a Gentleman   50
   Self-Portrait   49; Fig. 28

Photographic Credits

Andover Art Studio   Fig. 125
Mark C. Bisgrove Darkrooms Inc.   Fig. 90
E. Irving Blomstrann   Fig. 74
Lee Brian   Fig. 41
Will Brown   Fig. 42
Geoffrey Clements Photography   Fig. 112
A.C. Cooper Ltd.   Fig. 101
Coulthard Photography   Fig. 145
George M. Cushing Photography   Fig. 133
Frick Art Reference Library   Figs. 77, 106, and 122
Helga Photo Studio, Inc.   Fig. 135
Hughes Co.   Fig. 89
Eugene Mantie   Figs. 9, 14, 55, 85, and 125
O.E. Nelson   Fig. 30
Photo Studios Ltd.   Fig. 75
Rowles Studio   Fig. 93
Joseph Szaszfai   Figs. 62 and 63
Unusual Films Photographic Studios   Fig. 68
Herbert P. Vose   Figs. 37 and 52
J. White & Son   Fig. 70
A.J. Wyatt   Fig. 4